T0287158

"Len's book came at the perfect time for me. I've been thinking a lot about my legacy and the kind of lasting impact I want to make on the world. In *Self Less*, Len demonstrates through his own powerful, personal, and sometimes emotional stories about his life and development as a leader, that selfless leadership does indeed work. In fact, it can help to move mountains and inspire others to dream their own big dreams. Compelling story. Practical advice. Perfect timing for me and the world. Buy this book today, read it as soon as possible, and start applying its brilliant wisdom today."

**Jack Canfield**

Coauthor of the *New York Times* bestselling *The Success Principles*™: *How to Get from Where You Are to Where You Want to Be;* Coauthor of the #1 *New York Times* bestselling *Chicken Soup for the Soul*® series; Founder, Transformational Leadership Council

"*Self Less* is not an easy read. Not a quick read. And that is intended to be the ultimate compliment. I've read dozens of leadership books that one can flip through, pick up a clever one-liner here and there, and then get on with life. My advice: Make *Self Less* a slow—even very slow—read. Pause, contemplate, nod, frown, and get your head into the right place. Do those things, time and again, and this may well end up as the best leadership book you've ever read. It damn well made me pause again and again, think, and nod, and frown, and reflect. Wish I'd read it twenty years ago! Thanks, Len."

**Tom Peters**

Business Management Guru; Bestselling Author of twenty classic books, including the groundbreaking, *In Search of Excellence*

"Len's message in *Self Less* parallels my transformation where, though a series of revelations, the lens through which I saw our 12,000 global team members was completely reversed. My business education and professional experience caused me to see the people in our organization as "functions for my success." But, like Len, a family experience caused my lens to completely change, and I saw the team members as someone's precious child rather than an engineer or production worker.

Len clearly was impacted by his sense of responsibility to his children, and I have always said that parenting and leadership are identical. It is the sense of responsibility for those in your span of care  at home and where we work. The result is a dramatic shift from a *me* focus to a *we* focus where we embrace the profound responsibility of leadership.

Embracing Len's message in *Self Less* is the key to addressing the "poverty of dignity" we are seeing in the world where people feel used to achieve someone else's goal, rather than cared for as they work together to achieve mutual objectives. The world Len and I imagine is truly a society where people think of others first."

**Robert Chapman**
Chairman of the Board and CEO, Barry-Wehmiller Companies;
Bestselling Author, *Everybody Matters: The Extraordinary Power of Caring for Your People Like Family*

"This book is chock full of insights from a lifelong leadership student, teacher and practitioner. Mark Twain famously quipped, "I didn't have time to write a short letter, so I wrote a long one instead." Len has taken the time here to thoughtfully and concisely pen what's needed for a leader to reach the peak of the organizational pyramid; be it in academics, commerce, nonprofits, or civic life. Immediately after devouring it, I sent a copy to each of my kids. This sage guide will serve them—and you—well."

**Bob Eckert**
Chairman Emeritus, Mattel, Inc.

"Len's personal stories of selfless leadership and its role in organizational change are both engaging and inspiring. His approach mirrors very closely the leadership style my family has followed, and I think that both my dad and his good friend and colleague, Peter Drucker, would have wholeheartedly approved."

**Junro Ito**
Senior Managing Executive Officer,
Representative Director, Seven & I Holdings; 1989 Graduate of the
Peter F. Drucker and Masatoshi Ito School of Management,
Claremont Graduate University

"Len does more than talk about putting others first—he shows how he has learned selflessness over decades of leadership. In reflecting on his auspicious career in higher education, Len has distilled key lessons that tomorrow's leaders will need to succeed. His life stories beautifully underscore the power of perseverance and the joy of helping others flourish."

**Linda A. Livingstone**
President, Baylor University

"Len Jessup offers lessons on leadership in a highly readable story emphasizing teamwork and the benefits of finding success for everyone. Selfless leadership offers a path forward in the modern world of division and polarization."

**G. Gabrielle Starr**
President, Philip and Gertrude McConnell Professor of Human Relations, Pomona College

# SELF
# LESS

# SELF LESS

LESSONS LEARNED
FROM A LIFE DEVOTED
TO SERVANT LEADERSHIP,
*IN FIVE ACTS*

## LEN JESSUP, PhD

**Forbes** | Books

Published by Forbes Books, Charleston, South Carolina.
An imprint of Advantage Media Group.

Forbes Books is a registered trademark, and the Forbes Books colophon is a trademark of Forbes Media, LLC.

Printed in the United States of America.

10  9  8  7  6  5  4  3  2  1

ISBN: 979-8-88750-447-6 (Hardcover)
ISBN: 979-8-88750-448-3 (eBook)

Library of Congress Control Number: 2023920849

Cover design by Lance Buckley.
Layout design by Wesley Strickland.

This custom publication is intended to provide accurate information and the opinions of the author in regard to the subject matter covered. It is sold with the understanding that the publisher, Forbes Books, is not engaged in rendering legal, financial, or professional services of any kind. If legal advice or other expert assistance is required, the reader is advised to seek the services of a competent professional.

Since 1917, Forbes has remained steadfast in its mission to serve as the defining voice of entrepreneurial capitalism. Forbes Books, launched in 2016 through a partnership with Advantage Media, furthers that aim by helping business and thought leaders bring their stories, passion, and knowledge to the forefront in custom books. Opinions expressed by Forbes Books authors are their own. To be considered for publication, please visit **books.Forbes.com**.

*This story is dedicated to Kristi, Jamie, David, and other close friends and family members, without whom none of this would have happened, nor would it have meant so much.*

# CONTENTS

# PROLOGUE

*Wag more, bark less.*

**TO ME, THIS ADAGE** always meant I needed to be nicer to others by barking and growling less. Plus it seemed like a good mantra for life. But it was only later that I realized it was also an effective mantra for *leadership*.

As I evolved into leadership roles, I realized that while "wag more, bark less" was a key ingredient of good leadership, it didn't go far enough. In addition to being nice and less grouchy, I also needed to improve the way I thought about others. I needed to consider *their* wants, *their* fears, and *their* aspirations.

Rather than solely think about *my* goals, I needed to consider why my teammates and I were on this journey and what they wanted to achieve from it. In short, I needed to do more with others and think of myself less.

# When Were You at Your Best?

This concept crystalized for me at a recent leadership retreat I typically hold for my teams just before the start of each year.

I often collaborate with other people as I establish the format for these retreats. And this year I worked with a terrific doctoral student, Jen, who is studying positive organizational psychology and evaluation sciences. Jen is wrapping up her dissertation and has her own consulting business doing various forms of organizational development. Jen and I have taught and published together, and she is great to work with. Not only is she great at what she does, but she is smart as well. And so I thought it would be good to ask her to help me with the retreat. This turned out to be a smart move!

Jen helped me map out an effective agenda, and she led several exercises for the participants. We had a lot of new people in the group, and we also had individuals from all over the organization who weren't familiar with one another. Our goal for the introductions was to bring people together by creating an exercise that would clearly establish we were in a safe space and give participants the freedom to be themselves.

For the introductory exercise, Jen asked all thirty participants to privately reflect on a moment in their lives when they felt they were living as their best self. This moment could come from a pivotal time at work or a key instance in their personal lives. After identifying this moment and having the group reflect, Jen instructed us to jot down a few notes about this moment, which everyone would use to introduce themselves to the group. What unfolded was truly remarkable.

As fellow participants, Jen recommended that she and I go first. And so both of us shared some personal examples that helped participants loosen up. It took over an hour to finish this exercise, and while this was longer than our previous retreat introductions, this instance didn't bother me. In fact, I was ecstatic. The exercise was perfect, powerful, raw, emotional, helpful, and instructive. It allowed team members to get to know one another, and it opened the room as a space for trust and mutual respect. And it helped set the tone for the rest of the retreat.

Many of the moments described by participants were an anecdote about serving others. Some shared moments that occurred in their professional settings, while others shared moments that occurred in their personal settings. The stories were moving, and numerous participants fought back tears as they shared. What surprised me was how open they were at telling captivating personal stories. I'd never realized so many of our extended leadership team members were driven in this way.

Perhaps the most helpful part of this exercise was when I shared my moment privately with Jen beforehand. As everyone jotted down their personal notes, Jen and I quickly shared our moments with each other. As I spoke, I was embarrassed by my emotional response and told her I might not be able to tell this story to the entire team. But Jen, as always, was very encouraging and asked me to give it a go.

So I went ahead and told my story, and as I did, the tears were tough to hide. While there were many professionally highlighted moments I could have shared, my mind went to a moment that happened on a night nearly twenty years before. This moment was about as personal as it gets and one that had professional implications as well.

# The Lowest Moment of My Life

I had recently divorced and was living in northern Idaho at a beautiful home on Moscow Mountain, which my family and I affectionately referred to as the "mountain house."

At that point post-divorce, my weekly schedule included keeping our two young children for several days each week. This routine was a tough adjustment, and most days followed a similar pattern. After finishing work over at the Washington State University, I picked my kids up at their after-school program, shepherded them home, and prepped dinner while they played in an adjacent room.

After eating, the kids would do their traditional "thank the cook" by helping me clean up the kitchen. Then, they would have some playtime, homework, and cleanup for bed while I thought about which bedtime story to read with them (or to make up for them). I loved that routine, even though I'm not sure how I found the strength. I certainly could not do it now as I don't have nearly enough energy left in my reserves. But back then, life was different, and I wouldn't trade those evenings for the world. I later had my mom and one of my sisters help me, but in the early days, it was just me.

One night, just after I'd tucked them into bed and double-checked to make sure they were asleep, I breathed a sigh of relief and went in search of a nice Cabernet I'd hidden in the pantry. Pouring myself a glass and heading upstairs into the loft, I looked out the window and oversaw the stunning views below.

Peering out the large windows that overlooked the town of Moscow, I looked through the many pine trees surrounding my home and watched the sun set to my right. As I did, I enjoyed an unobstructed view into the valley, with the outline of the University of Idaho's Kibbie Dome still visible amid the twinkling lights of the town.

Taking a few sips of my Washington Cabernet, two strong emotions washed over me. The first was an incredibly powerful, deep sense of loneliness. I'm not talking about the garden variety feeling of being lonely, where you think to yourself, *Gee, I feel like doing something with someone, and so, maybe I should reach out to a friend and set up a lunch.* Instead, I felt a deep, dark, painful, aching sense of loneliness—perhaps even bordering on despair. I had been warned about this by a good friend and mentor at the time, Lane. A few weeks before my divorce, Lane told me that these feelings were inevitable and that they would occur most often in the evenings when I was alone. Man, he was right.

Of course, I wasn't technically alone because I had my kids. But with them safely in bed and me still awake, I felt alone in that big ol' house without even a neighbor in sight. This was the first time in a long time that I hadn't been in a committed relationship, and I felt adrift, longing for any sense of intimacy with other adults.

The longer I sat and stared, the more tears streamed down my face, plopping like little drops of rain into my Cabernet. To make matters worse, I had the Coldplay song, "Fix You," playing in the background. "And the tears come streaming down your face, when you lose something you can't replace. When you love someone, but it goes to waste. Could it be worse?"

Had Coldplay written that damn song for me? It sure felt like it. I'm not sure I've ever felt as low as I did that evening, and I suspect it was the strong emotion of that evening that makes that moment resonate to this day.

But, on the other hand, there was a second strong emotion I felt that was more positive. I also experienced this powerful feeling of happiness and relief that my kids were there with me, asleep in their beds, and that they were happy, fed, peaceful, at rest, and safe.

I was happy and proud I had figured out, at least for the moment, how to manage being a single dad without any help. I was also happy my kids were in a reasonably good place psychologically post-divorce with both their mom and me. In short, my kids were in a good place, both literally and figuratively, and that brought me a sense of calm and peace.

## No Choice but to Be Selfless

So why do I think that moment stands out as a time I was at my best?

Well, I think that prior to this point, I was a selfish person, and there were times when I'd let my ego get the best of me. But after my divorce and spending half the time by myself taking care of my kids, I had no choice but to try to force myself to be less selfish and more selfless. This shift was anything but an easy transition.

That evening as I sat alone, I cried more than I ever had. But I also felt that in moments like this, and the subsequent similar evenings to follow, I was at my best. I was still doing a good job at work. And more important, I was doing a good job at home with my kids. Yes, I made some mistakes, but I had found a balance, and I was now thinking and acting for my kids.

Even now, as I recount these memories and type out those Coldplay lyrics, I've been fighting back tears. But despite the pain, I am thankful that Jen encouraged me to be vulnerable and share my story with others. It certainly helped my teammates at the retreat open up, and even more important, sharing my moment with others has helped me better understand myself.

# From Selfish to Selfless at Work

Coming to this understanding helps me reflect on the events leading up to that poignant moment at the mountain house.

The whole notion of selfish versus selfless became especially important to me when, as a business school faculty member, I was asked to chair a department of my peers. In this new role, I was responsible for others in my department and had to ensure they had what they needed to be successful.

If you're familiar with the world of academia, you know that as a faculty member, you almost function as an independent contractor. This means you need to score points. In the academy, that means receiving good teaching evaluations and tallying up good grants, contracts, and donations. This also involves earning great publications, rave reviews from those in your executive education courses, equally good reviews from the clients and organizations you consult for, and similar reviews on any of the service initiatives you lead.

It's all about *you*.

You're like an NBA player who needs to average a certain number of points, rebounds, and assists to justify his position on the team. An example of a key metric for faculty has long been the important research citation indices that show the extent to which others are referencing your work. These citation indices are used to rate or rank faculty around the world. And as the department chair, I still needed to post good numbers for myself on all those personal metrics, but I now needed and wanted to help other faculty do the same.

To drive this point home even further, I received another promotion that pushed me into even more selfless behavior. When I shifted for the first time into a dean role, I was now responsible for people across many departments. This meant my own research and teaching ground to a halt and took a back seat. Now more than ever, I had to make that mental shift from worrying about *my* metrics to helping others perform well on *their* metrics. As a new dean, I recall bragging with some alumni about the work of one of our great faculty members named Rick.

Rick was a successful business school faculty member in finance, and I held him and his work in high regard. One afternoon, a group of alumni were visiting campus, and part of their experience was to meet me as their new dean. While I was tempted to talk about some of my research I thought would be relevant to them, I realized that would be selfish. I also realized that given the background of these alumni, this group would likely have more interest in getting to know Rick and benefit more from his expertise than mine.

As I sold Rick to them, it dawned on me that I was making a necessary shift as a leader from promoting myself to promoting someone on my team. It felt good, though a little odd compared to what I had been used to doing. But it was the right thing to do for our team members, our alumni, and our university.

Before I continue, let me turn to a base definition of selfless. In this case, the definition of selfless is being concerned more with the desires of others than with one's own. I like that definition, but I think that selfless is different from "self less." Treating the word "self" as a verb, I was starting to "self less," to act less in my own self-interests and proactively do more for others. It was an act of volition. I changed my behavior to better help this one person and everyone in the organization.

While selfless is a passive state of being or state of mind, it doesn't mean much if it doesn't cause you to change your behavior. You also need to proactively "self less," meaning that you must manifest this aspiration in your actions. And over time, we might develop that as a habit or routine. In my case, that subtle shift helped shape my approach to leadership in fundamental ways.

There are several important lessons to learn from this simple story.

First, all effective leadership begins with a reflective self-discovery process. On the surface, this sounds like an oxymoron. *Len, you're saying that to "self" less as a leader, I need to first think more about myself?* Exactly. Now you're getting it!

To be a better leader, you need to first stop and think about why you are doing what you are doing. In fact, it's good to do this throughout your *entire* stint as a leader. Periodic reflection is healthy, appropriate, and necessary. It helps you to better understand your motivations and to hone them to be a more effective leader. As a leader, it's important to not lose sight of why you're doing what you are doing. When you think about why you lead and what you are trying to accomplish, one would hope you are trying to make a positive difference through helping others.

Next, you'll realize that you need to better understand the motivations of those on your team. Ultimately, you need to make it about *their* journey, and so try not to get lost in your own.

# SELF LESS LESSON:

## Self-Reflection Is Healthy, Appropriate, and Necessary.

To some, this talk of selfless leadership might sound like what Henry Kissinger described as the important role that humility plays in leadership. Perhaps even more popular is what Jim Collins referred to as "Level Five Leaders," the most highly evolved form of leadership. Collins reasoned that a Level Five Leader is one who exhibits a strong personal humility combined with strong professional will. He further argued that these leaders have an intense drive and ambition but are also able to maintain a healthy dose of self-awareness and put the needs of others before their own.

My sense of a truly selfless leader is that they do indeed have a strong sense of humility, are self-aware, and are thinking about others. Great selfless leaders, as I am describing them, go one step beyond Collins's Level Five and routinely act as if looking out for the best interests of others is a natural and reflexive response. I've found that this way of thinking is strongly embodied in the many works of Tom Peters, all the way from the groundbreaking *In Search of Excellence* and through much of his subsequent work on humanism in leadership.

Going back to my story about Rick, the other important lesson I discovered is that this isn't just a story about leading change in higher education. I say this because you might be tempted to think, *Sure, leading this way is important in higher ed because they have that concept of "shared governance" where faculty appropriately feel they are supposed to participate in decision-making for the university. Of course, you have to be self less in that setting. Otherwise you couldn't get anything done.*

*Not only that, but you also can't fire or force anything on faculty members because of the lifelong employment that tenure brings.*

Contrary to popular belief, in some instances, you *can* fire or redirect faculty members. Furthermore, shared governance doesn't necessarily mean the organization is run solely by faculty votes or mob rule. Universities are better than that and are more like other organizations than you think. That's not the point I'm making here, however. My point is that in any organizational setting—whether a university, corporation, government, or nonprofit—you need to include people rather than exclude them. You must help them help you co-create and share a vision, solicit good ideas, figure out the right way to go about doing something, and secure their buy-in on initiatives.

This isn't just something that happens in academe. Thankfully, this is beginning to happen everywhere.

→ Less top down and more bottom up

→ Less autocratic and more democratic

→ Less hierarchical and more flat and lean

→ Less exclusionary and more inclusive

→ Less proprietary and more collaborative

→ Less closed and more open

→ Less about being the smartest person at the table and more about surrounding yourself with people smarter than you

→ Less about the leader with the vision and more about a shared vision

→ Less about the leader fulfilled personally and instead more about a team fulfilled *together*

## SELF LESS LESSON:

## Selfless Leadership Is Needed and Works in Any Setting.

Now, as you read you might be thinking, *This all sounds like it would take forever to get things done. If I've got to stop what I'm doing and think about others first, this will really slow me down. Besides, I've got hundreds of people who report to me, and if I speak with everyone (or even just their supervisors), that's going to take forever.*

I can see how you would think this way. But just the opposite is true. Think this through, and you'll see what I mean.

Consider that problem you think you've already got figured out. You probably think that you don't need other people's input. Now ask yourself this question: *What if I am wrong?* If you are, after you forge ahead with your vision, you'll have to reverse gears and restart. And this will take longer because you are now backtracking. Worse, you'll have lost people's trust and confidence.

Alternatively, you can make fast decisions and do a quick check-in with some key unit leaders. But while taking this shortcut will seemingly get you to implementation faster, the trouble is you'll likely see passive-aggressive resistance along the way because you haven't established the buy-in you're going to need. You also risk the possibility you still don't have a handle on the right approach to the changes that need to be made.

Thankfully, there is a better way.

Through personal experience, I've discovered my teams will move faster and go farther when they use the approach I've described earlier. Because my teams made sure we received the right input, we built strong buy-in for the solution and implementation. This minimized resistance, and we were able to better engage people in the implementation.

I think this is exactly why we have been able to move so fast, do so much, and go so far with people feeling good about the changes. A simple way of saying this is, *Go slow to go fast*. Practically speaking, if you are a leader, be less of a *sage on the stage* and more of a *guide on the side*.

## SELF LESS LESSON:

### Selfless Leadership Doesn't Slow You Down.

To summarize these lessons, it's important to be more introspective and better understand what makes you tick as a leader. Then you can better engage your teammates and lead them toward a shared vision. Even better, you can do this regardless of your position or setting.

And another thought for you. When I think back on my decision to promote Rick's story over my own, it wasn't as if a lightbulb popped on in my mind and I suddenly thought more about others than I did myself. Instead, I think this mindset started for me at an early age. While my curriculum vitae lists my stints as university president at the top and works backward to my time as a community college student and athlete, to put my life in context, this list should start with my childhood. The seemingly ordinary, day-to-day experiences of youth are not just memories. They are the foundational ingredients that shape a life.

Everything that now defines me was created and honed at a very early age. This includes characteristics and attributes such as:

→ accepting and giving unconditional love,

→ feeling intense drive and a need for hard work,

→ sometimes lacking confidence and feeling imposter syndrome,

→ feeling a strong sense of gratitude,

→ strongly wanting to have a positive influence on others,

→ often engaging in healthy introspection,

→ wanting to serve others in a greater purpose, and

→ having a willingness to take chances.

## SELF LESS LESSON:

### Selfless Leadership Doesn't Happen Overnight.

If there is anything I hope my story does, it's to prompt you to reflect on how *you became you*.

My upbringing shaped my personality and who I became as a leader. It also shaped my goals, causing me to want to make a difference with others. That led me to take on bigger and bigger leadership challenges in organizations that needed transformation. Along the way, I developed into a selfless leader, literally trying to self less, but yet needing to lead people to do some seemingly impossible things.

Thus, this book is about selfless leadership as a way to lead others in transformational organizational change. Yes, this sounds counter-intuitive. After all, aren't great leaders supposed to take charge and tell people what to do? While I know it's natural to think this way, just the opposite is true. Selfless leading helped me and others to do some amazing things together. Selfless leadership was and is for me a powerful way to lead others in some amazing, transformational organizational changes.

So that's the central plot here: *selfless leadership as a powerful tool for leading others through transformational organizational changes.*

In order to delve into this idea, I will share a series of personal examples to illustrate my points. From there, I'll use that foundation to describe how those moments shaped my approach to leadership. And then I'll drive home these points by sharing stories about how teams I've led accomplished some wonderful objectives.

Oh, and just for fun, I'm going to loosely follow the five-act structure for ancient plays. My hope is this centuries-old approach to storytelling challenges you to rethink the way you run your life and lead your teams. And perhaps best of all, this book is an easy read, and you'll likely get through it in an hour or less.

With that said, let the opening act commence!

# ACT 1:

# ORIGINS

*Do you ever think about where you came from, how that shaped you, and why that's important to you now?*

**I CAME FROM** a long line of Italians on both sides of my family, with my mom's side from the Aeolian Islands off Sicily and my dad's side from the area near Trieste, just east of Venice. My ancestors, who scratched out a living by commercial fishing and other forms of physically demanding labor, immigrated to the United States circa 1900 to escape oppression—a story writ large by the millions who came through Ellis Island and other ports of entry. They left the only life they had ever known, facing huge risks and sacrifices, to find a better life in America for kids and grandkids they did not yet have.

My dad was a fireman, and I've never known anyone who worked as hard as him. Sadly, he played hard as well, smoking and drinking for much of his life. He also had a bad temper, and so us kids walked on eggshells around him during the rare moments he was home. He simply wore out his heart and died at sixty-five while undergoing his second major bypass surgery. He was the epitome of the adage, "The candle that burns twice as bright, burns half as long."

As a child, I tried hard to please him and constantly sought his affirmation. I realize now that much of my adult life was spent trying to measure up to him—trying hard to please the ornery, ill-tempered Italian who never seemed to like me.

My dad shaped me by his absence, his fleeting approval, and his temper, whereas my mom shaped me by constantly being there for me and my younger brother while reinforcing belief in ourselves and our capabilities. She instilled lessons, manners, and respect. But perhaps her greatest impact on us was that she openly loved and adored us. Where my dad was like a roiling pot ready to boil over at any moment, my mom was like a cozy fireplace that always made us feel good.

Dad and I occasionally talked about cars and motorcycles during my senior years in high school, but there was little talk of college. By this point, I'd made some good friends at high school, and they were going to college. My best friend, Craig, was headed to Cal State Chico and wanted me to join him. My dad, however, strongly advised me to think about getting a good civil service job like he had with the fire department down in the Bay Area—complete with health benefits and retirement. There I was, coming of age, wanting to head off to college with my friends, and my dad was having none of it. I felt frustrated, disappointed, and unsure.

Truth be told, I didn't feel confident enough to follow my friends to the university. Instead, I targeted the local community college because it seemed more feasible, and I also wanted to see if I could make the baseball team. My dad reluctantly agreed to let me go because, to him, continuing to play baseball seemed like a reasonable thing for me to do.

So off I went, hoping to make the team and thinking I would get a two-year certificate in business administration and return to Fort Jones to find a civil service job that would allow me to work for one of the local businesses or farms. And make the team I did, learning a lot from being a student-athlete in the process.

That said, one of the more impactful moments happened in my studies, but perhaps not in the way you might expect.

# Confidence Shaken to the Core

When I entered the college, the bad news was that there was so much I didn't understand. But the good news was that I had a voracious appetite to learn. I'd always enjoyed reading and writing in grade school, but this added challenge was wonderful. I loved every course, every topic, and even got paid to tutor.

My baseball coach was also my advisor, and I remember the day I told him about my plan to get a business administration certificate and go back home to work. He smiled, shook his head, and suggested I work on my general education courses so that I could transfer along with some of my friends to one of the Cal State schools. My coach saw my capabilities in the classroom and believed I was destined for bigger and better things off the playing field. And who was I to argue with him?

But though my coach believed in me, others did not. I recall the time I wrote an extensive paper for my art history class. I spent countless hours strategizing, researching related works in the library, and crafting a compelling story I believed my professor would like.

I submitted my paper, and a few days later, the professor asked me to remain after class to discuss what I'd written. Nervously, I followed him to his office, not sure what he would say. Once we stepped inside, he closed the door and accused me of cheating. He said the paper was too well-done for me to have written it. I was flabbergasted, and it took me a moment to gather my wits. Here I was, feeling unqualified to be in college, and a professor I respected was saying my work was too good to be true. I wasn't sure whether to cry, get angry, storm out of his office, or leave campus altogether.

But I gathered myself and swore to my professor that I had written the paper. I insisted I could prove it if he gave me a chance. And for the next few minutes, he placed me under the microscope, questioning my logic, debating my line of argument, and asking why I had chosen this or that reference. It felt like going through a dissertation defense, except that I was a naïve freshman, completely inexperienced in this environment, and not sure if this guy was going to have me kicked out of school.

After several minutes, the professor finished grilling me, apologized, and said that my paper was very well-written and that he was now certain it was indeed my work. Walking out of his office, I left in a cloud of mixed emotions. I was unsure whether to be mad at him for initially not believing in me or elated in his newfound confidence that I was the real deal. In any event, I felt so relieved and left his office feeling affirmed. Perhaps I *could* succeed at college, and perhaps I deserved to be there.

## SELF LESS LESSON:

### Don't Let 'Em Bring You Down.

After finishing two years of college, I followed my friends down to Chico State. The difference now was that I wasn't going to play baseball. I was going purely to attend classes, and my dad wasn't happy about it.

He complained I was going to be wasting time and money at that "damn college." But I was determined to keep going and was excited about my future. In fact, when I arrived at Chico State, I was like a kid in a candy store. Once again, I loved every course, every professor, and every moment. Now I was exposed to even smarter people, interacted with faculty members who were active experts in their fields, and had the luxury to access a massive library.

It was daunting, and I was still unsure of myself. Some days I struggled with imposter syndrome. But fortunately, with each passing day, I gained more confidence.

Then *it* happened again.

Because I was so curious about everything and couldn't settle on a major, I opted for Information and Communication Studies. This was an interdisciplinary degree that allowed me to take classes in everything I liked, including business, computer science, communications, and social sciences. I excelled in every class until I ran into a communications professor who, much like with the professor back at the community college, didn't believe I had written one of my papers. This time, though, I was ready. He called me to his office and had a colleague with him to grill me.

I was able to quickly dispel their skepticism about the authenticity of the paper, and this time around I wasn't shocked or even surprised. Instead, I was more curious and intellectual about it, wondering why these professors incorrectly surmised that I wasn't smart and couldn't write. I figured that because I didn't often speak in class, and because I typically dressed and looked like a jock, they just assumed I couldn't write. It made me think about how I was showing up in class and in life and that I needed to work harder at letting people know who I was and where I was headed.

I realized something else. By that point, there had been so many people who doubted me along the way: teachers, professors, coaches, colleagues, and even my own dad. And I became determined not to let their perceptions, doubts, or sense of my limits define me or hold me back. I reasoned that they were limited in what they really knew about me, and they were biased by their own issues, opinions, life experiences, and views of the world.

I didn't take it personally. At an even more basic level, I vowed that I wasn't going to give them that power over me. I knew what I was capable of, and that was enough for me. They would see, in time, who I was. And if they didn't, so be it.

## SELF LESS LESSON:

### Don't Let Them Take Away Your Power over Yourself.

After two years at Chico State, I finished up my undergraduate degree in fine style. And those same two faculty members who grilled me over my paper became friends and let me know I was among the top students graduating in that major. I was proud I had completed the program and done well.

Sadly, my dad didn't seem too impressed with any of it and did not attend my graduation. All I remember from that day was that it was hot and sweat poured from my forehead as I stood alongside other graduates on the football field in my cap and gown. But by then, no amount of negativity could deter me, and all I could think about was what was next.

I went through interviews for career positions that final spring of my undergraduate program, and I had several decent job offers. But none of them lit my fire. Based on encouragement from the faculty members, I investigated a master's degree. Because I had been at Chico State for only two years, I decided to stay for an MBA so that I could enjoy the university and college town atmosphere a bit longer.

My parents could do little to help me pay for my education, so I worked multiple jobs every summer, as well as a part-time job on campus during each school year. Back at home that summer, it appeared my dad had taken the attitude that I must be doing something right because I was now at least studying business. He didn't say much, but he stopped saying anything negative to me about going to college. That was certainly a relief. He wasn't encouraging, but at least he wasn't disparaging.

## Turning the Corner with My Dad

I loved my MBA program because it was so useful and practical. Along the way, I made several close new friends and excelled in my courses. Thankfully, there were no more cheating accusations from faculty members. In fact, I became the equivalent of class president my second year and developed great relationships with my professors, often having dinner with them and the occasional meet-up at one of the local bars.

They provided lots of useful, encouraging advice, and several of them urged me to think about going on for a doctorate in business after my MBA. One faculty member in particular, Bernie, was instrumental in guiding me into my subsequent doctoral studies. While I had no idea what a PhD was, let alone what one did with it, I trusted his judgment.

Bernie was anal, demanding, and sometimes cranky. He held very high standards, but he was also very helpful and never let me slack off. Bernie was quick to offer constructive criticism and was brutal in editing my draft papers and master's thesis. He's long since passed away, but I still think of him. And when I do, I look to the sky and thank him for the impact he had on my life.

By the time I finished my MBA, my dad's attitude about me attending school had completely shifted. I'll never forget my MBA graduation. This time, both my parents attended. And when one of my faculty mentors said to my dad, "You must be so incredibly proud of your son," Dad replied, "You know, we cannot comprehend what he is doing, but it is obviously working out well for him, and we're supportive of it."

I remember this line because my dad never used words like "comprehend." It also stuck out for me because that was literally the first time I recalled ever hearing my dad say something positive about what I was doing in college. It floored me. Finally, he saw value in what I was doing and was affirming me.

Soon afterward I entered my doctoral program at the University of Arizona, an even larger and more research-oriented university that was farther from home. It had just become a member of the Association of American Universities and was one of the top sixty in the country. And there was a moment one morning at my parents' house in Fort Jones, California, that I'd never forget.

Everything was packed in my car and U-Haul trailer as I prepared to make the long drive to my new university and earn my PhD. My mom and dad got up early to see me off. After hugging my mom in the living room, she made me promise to drive safely and call her at each stop, as well as when I arrived at my destination, Tucson.

My dad walked me out and, in private out on the front porch, looked me in the eyes with a warm smile. Holding me by my arms, he somberly nodded and said, "You're off on a great adventure ..." and just kind of let the sentence hang there in the fresh mountain air on that sunny Northern California morning.

It wasn't much, but like his comment at my MBA graduation, it astonished me because he rarely said much and never expressed any emotions. That was as close as he ever got to opening up with me. I still get tears in my eyes just thinking about that moment.

## Off on a Great Adventure

I arrived at the University of Arizona two days later. It was a long, hot summer drive. Tired after two full days on the road, I pulled up with my U-Haul trailer in tow. Remembering I had a promise to keep, I immediately found a payphone in the lobby of the university library and called my mom. I had never lived so far from home, and I was lonely, didn't yet know where I would spend the night, and felt intimidated by this new, high-powered research university with an even smarter group of people around me.

As I spoke, I suspect my mom sensed I was holding back tears. I reassured her that everything was fine, that I was safe, and that I would quickly settle in to school. Truth be told, I was scared and homesick. I found my department within the business school and was relieved that the staff accepted me with open arms and treated me like family. Right away, I felt at ease.

They introduced me to the other doctoral students back in a "bullpen" area of small offices and cubicles. Everyone was nice, and one in particular, Shawn, let me stay at his place that first year. Two other fellow doctoral students soon became two of my closest friends. Mark was a kid from Phoenix, and Joe was from Great Falls, Montana. All three of us shared many similarities.

Every doctoral student was smart and helpful, including my two amigos, but aside from the three of us, nearly every one of the other doctoral students came from an impressive school—much better than my undergrad university. The faculty and department chair were even more intimidating, and I wondered what I had gotten myself into. Had I bitten off more than I could chew?

I had a serious case of imposter syndrome by that point, and it was made even worse when the supportive staff showed me my private personnel file in the department office. They weren't supposed to do that, but they obviously cared for me and wanted me to see that I'd gotten into the doctoral program by the skin of my teeth.

My grades and references from my faculty at Chico State were exceptionally good (particularly the letter from my cranky mentor, Bernie), but I could tell from the notes written about me in my file that my new faculty at this research university were not impressed with my undergraduate institution, nor were they impressed with my test scores. Though they admitted me, some were clearly dubious about my chances for success.

I had worked hard in prior summer jobs, for some of my tougher undergrad classes, and for my entire MBA program, but I had never worked as hard as I did during the four years of my doctoral program at the University of Arizona. It was insane, and it consumed my every waking hour.

When I did travel home, it was only for short holiday stays, and I typically worked on research projects during my entire visit. I felt that I had a lot to prove and that I had to outwork the other students from top undergrad schools and master's programs. I worked my tail off and, once again, loved every minute of it. It was the most stimulating, rewarding, beneficial, and transformative experience of my professional career. I knew then that I was destined for a "life of the mind" and would likely work on college campuses for the rest of my life.

## The Life of the Mind

I was growing intellectually and gaining more self-confidence, but I still had that lingering self-doubt. The upside was that it caused me to work even harder. My mantra became that *if a day goes by where I don't embarrass myself, I'm not trying hard enough.* I was surrounded by so many smart, talented people that I figured I was bound to say or do something embarrassing.

But I had to let that go. I knew that for me to continue to grow, I had to continue to learn and get better. Mistakes weren't likely going to be catastrophic. Rather, they were opportunities for learning and growth.

Fortunately, my dad was able to see me excel through my doctoral program and begin my career as a professor. He and my mom visited me often throughout my doctoral program and into my new job as a junior faculty member in the business school for which I initially worked. It was a great time of my life, growing and evolving personally and professionally.

I also felt that I had finally earned my dad's affirmation. He and I talked during their frequent visits and over short phone conversations. As we did, it became clear that he was genuinely happy and proud of me. I was into my early thirties at that point, but the wait was worth it. Finally, I had the affirmation I sought.

Dad told me I had scored the ultimate civil service job working at a state university because I only had to put in only a few hours a week teaching classes. He understood teaching, but to him, everything else I did outside the classroom didn't seem like work. For example, getting paid for reading, writing, thinking, sitting in meetings, and hanging out in my research lab with my "friends" all seemed like slack time to him. He and I would often get a laugh out of that, and I assured him I was working hard all the time.

## Shaped by My Past

I think back on this time in my life often and can see now how these events and people shaped me. Coaches, teachers, family members, and my parents molded me in those early formative years. I was shaped by my mom's constant love and support, just as I was shaped by my dad's frequent absence and relative lack of support. They have both left their indelible mark on me, and I benefited equally from both.

I also came to the poignant realization of just how important my grandparents and great-grandparents were. The sacrifices and risks they took in leaving Italy and coming to America had profound effects. They did it for me, a grandson they didn't yet have, to increase the chances that I would later succeed. In a sense, I had a debt to repay for the sacrifices they'd made. And through my hard work and success, I was going to show the deeply felt gratitude I had for them.

That thought about my ancestry always lingered at the edges of my mind, but it came into sharp focus several years ago with the help of a good friend and talented executive coach named Nancy. Like my ancestors, higher education transformed me in so many important ways, and I felt an obligation not only to my undergraduate and graduate universities but also to give back to the higher education system in general.

I've long felt a strong commitment to pay it forward by helping others have successful higher education experiences and the same opportunities I had. This is why I've dedicated my working life to higher education.

Somewhere in early adulthood, this all rang clear for me, and it shaped my life's purpose. A decade or so ago, I picked up a small notebook and wrote about my purpose in life. I still have that book in a nearby desk drawer. In it, I wrote, "When I get to the end of my path, I want to be able to look back and know in that moment that I did everything I possibly could, to do as much good as I possibly could, to have as much positive impact as I possibly could, for as many people as I possibly could, and that I never shied away from an opportunity to do so."

I would live a purpose-driven life in service to others. I would be a servant leader, and higher education would be my platform and vehicle. Furthermore, I would do it for my family, past, present, and future. That was my mission.

### SO, AS WE COME TO THE CLOSE OF ACT 1,

I ask you a question: *How do your origins influence your bearing and destination?* Do you think about where you are from, how your upbringing shaped you, and how it might affect where you're headed? Perhaps it is limiting you, and you should let it go. Or perhaps it is shaping you in positive ways, and you ought to lean into it.

# ACT TWO:
# BELIEFS

**WHAT ARE YOUR** *core beliefs and values?* What is truly important to you? How does that drive you or limit you? What are the core beliefs and values of those around you in your personal and professional lives? And as a leader, how might your understanding of your and your team's beliefs and values help you to lead, especially in times of change?

I remember a conversation with one of my toughest MBA professors as I was heading off to earn my doctorate. He was an ornery old fellow who taught management courses. In one of our conversations, he said I needed to be careful when I went down to the research university because the faculty and staff would want to pull me away from my studies and my research. They'd want me to do things for the department, school, or university. And he went on to say that if I agreed to their requests, this would get in the way of my work. I had no idea what he meant, and so I asked him to explain.

He politely shared, "For someone like you, they are going to want to trot you out to speak with this or that audience." He argued that

I didn't want to do too much of that and be turned into the poster boy for the school. Rather, I needed to focus on my work. I still didn't get what he meant and sheepishly asked if he would explain what he meant by "someone like me." He responded by pointing out that because I was "clean cut" and articulate, the faculty and staff would want to use me for promotions when I needed to focus on my learning.

He was right in the sense that I often was asked to be the spokesperson for our group of doctoral students and for our program. But when asked, I willingly agreed because I felt it was the right thing to do. I also often found myself in leadership roles throughout my doctoral program and in the early stages of my career. For example, I was asked to lead other doctoral students in the development and implementation of an executive education program on leadership and business management for nurses and staff at a local hospital, a gig that was deemed not lucrative enough for faculty.

## SELF LESS LESSON:

### Strongly Consider Accepting Even the Little Assignments.

On a similar note, early in my career as a faculty member, I was tasked with being a department chair. Older and more experienced faculty would have been much better for the role, but they were busy and didn't want to serve. They wanted me to do it, even though I was young and fresh out of my doctoral program. Some thought I might have been the youngest in that role at that university or even in that entire university system.

I never shied away from an opportunity to help, to speak up, or to lead, whether in informal or formal roles. It always felt that I was needed and that I could add value. More to the point, I believed it was the right thing to do. And as I kept saying yes to these opportunities, the roles and assignments got bigger, and the potential for impact became correspondingly larger. Within a relatively short time, I was offered roles that forged my skills and reputation as a leader and change agent. Some of these included participating in some major organizational turnarounds.

Early in my career, I was asked as a new dean to step in and help save a business school that was about to lose its AACSB accreditation. The catch was we had only twelve months to do it. A short time later, I was leading the foundation for that same university. It had fallen so far behind in fundraising that it needed to double its receipts just to catch up to competing schools. Our time frame for catching up? Two to three years. The president of the school also wanted to break through the $5 million ceiling for major gifts in addition to launching a billion-dollar comprehensive campaign. Let's just say it was a crazy three years!

Later in my career, I was recruited to be the dean of the business school where I had earned my doctorate. I could not help but wonder if they checked my transcripts and saw the notes in my personnel file from the faculty who didn't want to enroll me. In any event, they wanted me back, and I was happy to oblige. In that role, I was asked to help them maintain their climb in rankings while also figuring out how to become a self-sustaining entity on campus. In the words of Jim Collins, this one was a classic "good to great" organizational transformation.

Shortly thereafter, I was asked to lead a dynamic university in its quest to become a Carnegie R1 research university, to launch a medical school, and to find a way to build a football stadium without having to pay for it. The time frame to complete these projects? Yesterday.

To some, I'm sure my career resembles a circuitous pathway, with lots of moving around the country from one job to the next. They're not wrong. In fact, after one of my moves, I was ranked number 1 in the *Chronicle of Higher Education*'s ranking of the most "high contrast" moves made that year by university leaders. I received this ranking after I left UNLV, a large, upstart, urban, dynamic public university, to lead Claremont Graduate University (CGU), a small private school steeped in history in a beautiful little college town in Southern California.

However, having lived through all those moves, I can tell you that with each transition, I moved into a larger or more challenging leadership role. It was as though I felt called into those roles in a compelling way. At times, I was literally getting a new assignment from my boss. And in other cases, I was recruited by either another university's board or a search firm contracted to help them fill their position.

Each of those moves made total sense to me in the moment, and each felt like it was exactly the next thing I was supposed to do to achieve my life's purpose. Time and again, I would turn to that small notebook in my desk drawer and reflect on what I had written, "When I get to the end of my path …"

With a lot of hard work, a little luck, and the help of many amazing people along the way, we were able to accomplish what we had set out to do in each of those examples highlighted previously. It is remarkable when I look back on it. I am grateful in so many ways for everything I've been able to participate in and all the insights I gleaned. I can point to:

→ the importance of co-creating a vision;

→ inclusiveness in building a credible, useful strategic plan for how to get the organization from point A to point B;

→ carefully selecting and visiting benchmark universities and learning from them;

→ surrounding myself every day with people smarter than me;

→ making shared governance work for everyone;

→ engaging great board members and putting them to work for us;

→ figuring out how to work around board members who were dysfunctional;

→ rallying the community and other friends of the university in support of us;

→ working with the governor and legislature to advance the entire state; and

→ the power of corporate partnerships when done right.

## SELF LESS LESSON:

### Take on Big Challenges, but Do So with Eyes Wide Open.

My list of leadership lessons could fill volumes. However, what stands out for me is much more simple, personal, and at the fundamental level of how people behave.

Think about what leadership is at its core. The most elemental definition is that it is the ability to influence others' thinking and actions. A good leader, by definition, can influence the way people think and act.

A leader might simply be trying to get people to perform tasks in a certain way, under certain constraints, and within a prescribed time. On the other end of the spectrum, a leader might be tasked with trying to move an entire organization from an undesirable "as is" situation to a "to be" state in the future that is better.

In all cases, a leader must get things done with and through other people. So, at its core, leadership is fundamentally about leading change, leading people through change, and motivating people to collectively enact that change.

## SELF LESS LESSON:

### Leadership Is Organizational Change.

Think about leaders who find themselves in a situation where they must move an entire organization from where it is now to where it really needs to be. That is some difficult, complex, and yet exciting stuff. And it's also where great leaders emerge and earn their pay.

Imagine you're now tasked with moving hundreds, thousands, or tens of thousands of people all in the same direction to a desired state for the organization. All of them are at different levels of motivation. They each possess different skills and abilities, with contrasting ideas about the organization's needs and direction. Some of them work actively against the change, some are onboard, while others jump ship. All the while, your competitors are hoping and perhaps helping you to slip up along the way. Talk about a grand challenge!

I could share numerous stories about what I've learned in leading change that either did or didn't work. But my purpose here is to simply ask you to think about where to start if you find yourself tasked with leading a robust organizational change. Where should you begin?

Think back again to that basic definition of leadership: *to influence the way that people think or act.* With that in mind, maybe you find yourself in a position where you need to influence people to do something. You might *think* you know what it is they need to do and the direction you need them to move, but don't be so certain.

Are you sure you are right about the direction in which you want them to move, what you want them to do, and why you want them to do it? At this early stage, if you're convinced you're right about the change needed, you're probably wrong. That's where you need to begin.

You need to figure out what the problem is and confirm it with the people who are involved and impacted. How do they see things? I always begin any organizational change by assuming I do not know much of anything about what is actually happening in the organization, about its current state, and about what the desired state should be. Because I always assume I don't know anything, I always begin by listening, learning, asking a lot of questions, and talking with as many people as I possibly can.

## SELF LESS LESSON:

### Listen before You Speak or Make Up Your Mind.

In nearly every one of the organizational transformations I've led, I've enlisted the aid of Bill, a dear friend and professional organizational development expert who is great with people and successively led his own management consulting firm.

In addition to advising me as I began these transformations, Bill would also meet privately on my behalf with relevant stakeholders, people both within and external to the organization. He would interview each of them and solicit their candid feedback about how things were going and what needed to happen next.

I've often found that when I talk directly with people as I'm heading into the organization as the new leader, they either cannot or will not be totally honest with me. This is why you should consider having someone else help you on your listening tour. Whether you talk with people directly or someone else helps you listen to others, you are going to need to learn from the people impacted by the change about to happen.

From all that learning, you will get to the point where you have a good sense of what you think the current state of the organization is, what the real problems are, why they are happening, how they are holding the organization back, what the desired state of the organization is, how that can be enacted, where the opponents and hot spots are, where the change agents are, and so on. You won't have the complete picture, and it will likely morph over time, but through this learning phase, you will have a much better handle on things than when you started.

# SELF LESS LESSON:

## You've Got to Size It Up, before You Take It On.

So, you've listened, you've learned, and you've gained at least an initial basic sense of what needs to happen. Your next step is to ensure that the relevant people involved see clearly and consistently that there is a need for change and what that change needs to be.

If they don't see the need for change, your efforts will not work. You might not get all of them initially, but you've got to have most of the people seeing roughly the same thing with the same intensity. There are also inevitably a few key influencers in the group who need to be onboard—in my case, this has been a key board member, a trusted dean, a midlevel manager, a well-known and influential senior faculty member, or a clear top performer. These key influencers will be important to effecting change because others will look to them for their opinions and actions.

While the first step was all about listening, this next step is both listening and communicating. You and your team, including those key influencers, will need to work together to explain, persuade, cajole, negotiate, prove, incentivize, and, yes, sometimes plea with others involved. You'll need to make sure the coalition of the willing is large enough and strong enough so that you've created sufficient wind at your back to counter any resistance you're likely to face. With any luck, you've now got a clearer sense of the opposition and how you need to contend with them as well.

These organizational transformations are often grounded in very simple values. Sometimes these values will vary among people within the organization to the extent that the values are clear, shared, or salient. In any event, these values exist as basic truths for people in the organization, things they think are important to them as members of this organization and that guide their behavior.

More to the point, these values can either propel or hinder the changes. In most cases, the changes I've been involved in invoked fundamental values such as the pursuit of excellence, self-sufficiency, or helping others who were less fortunate. In unproductive organizational cultures, these values may be expressed in negative ways, like everyone out for themselves, keep your head down, or outlast the leader.

The trick for me was distilling these values to their core tenets. From there, I communicated both the good and the bad and rallied people around the productive values while sidelining the negative ones, until enough people were onboard to begin moving the organization forward. In this part of the process, I spent a lot of time appealing to what individuals like Abraham Lincoln call their "better angels."

## SELF LESS LESSON:

### In This Case, Values and Organizational Culture Will Eat Strategy for Breakfast, Lunch, and Dinner.

Even more fundamental, however, was the hard work of convincing people that it was indeed possible to shift the organization forward. Let me be clear. Nearly everything else I've said until now is straightforward, doable, and easy compared to what I'm about to say.

You want to know the most difficult aspect of organizational transformations? It's convincing people that the vision you are presenting is possible. Once you've done this, everything gets a lot easier.

When people think something isn't possible, it's hard to move to the next level with them. Without at least a glimmer of hope, they will struggle to proceed. I've often found this to be the most difficult part of the organizational change process, especially if you're trying to take people to a new level or into areas they've never been before.

What seems daunting often is (at least until you identify and change critical limiting beliefs). A limiting belief is a state of mind that you might have, or a belief about yourself or your situation, that restricts you in some way. Jack Canfield, for example, has written and spoken extensively about self-limiting beliefs and the adverse effects they can have on people. Changing people's beliefs about what is possible for them and their organization is perhaps the most difficult component of leadership.

To illustrate this point, let me share a personal example.

# No Way We Are Going to Get This Done

For much of my early career as a faculty member, I had a goal to be in an endowed chair position at a good school out West (preferably in a college town with great access to outdoor activities and in a good place to raise kids). I worked tirelessly toward that goal.

Thankfully, Joe, one of the amigos from my doctoral program, recruited me and our other close friend, Mark, to join him at Washington State University (WSU), to help build and grow a nascent information systems program in the business school. It was great to have the band back together again, and we often refer to those days as our Camelot. Together we worked hard to build a top-ranked program, loving every minute of the process. I had achieved everything professionally that I had set out to do up until that moment.

But then things changed.

The prior dean had left, and we found ourselves with interim leadership, facing what we all knew was going to be a difficult reaccreditation bid with the AACSB—one of the primary business school accreditation agencies. My team in the information systems program felt that someone internally needed to throw their hat in the ring for the dean's job, just in case the national search for outside candidates turned up empty. My colleagues in my department encouraged me to go for it. I went ahead and had a long talk with Alberto, the head of the search firm (another fellow who has become a lifelong friend and mentor), and I applied for the job shortly thereafter. I then learned the truth behind the adage, "Be careful what you wish for."

As I typically did, I challenged myself and my assumptions about whether I thought I could handle this new role. I spoke with my mentors, colleagues, friends, and family and slowly built the support and confidence I needed to take on the new role. I remember reading that Wharton, one of the best business schools in the country, had just hired a new dean who was my same age (forty-one), and this gave me added confidence. I figured that if this man could do it at a top business school, then I could surely do it at my business school.

In my first day on the job, I was barraged by my new staff with a host of problems. Several things were broken in terms of the way the business school operated. Many of our alumni and other external stakeholders had disengaged, and our finances were problematic on several dimensions. Worst of all, we were on probation and about to lose our AACSB accreditation.

My new staff presented me with an accreditation report including a list of twenty-six major items that needed to be fixed before the external accreditation review team (deans from other business schools) would recommend to the AACSB that we should be reaccredited. Even worse, we had only twelve months left on the clock to make these changes. It kind of felt like someone was pushing smelling salts in front of my face and snapping me into a new reality.

As I read the report, I realized these suggested improvements were not *minor* items. Nearly every one of them involved a significant organizational change in and of itself. For example, our admissions process was broken, and so an entirely new system needed to be built and followed. Our annual tenure and promotion process was also not being followed, and instead these decisions seemed to be driven more by politics. Every item on that list was just as big and difficult as fixing admissions and fixing the tenure and promotion process.

I was staggered that people hadn't been more forthright about these problems and about our accreditation teetering in the balance. I was on the leadership team as a department chair, and, surprisingly, I had not yet heard this level of detail about the depth and breadth of the accreditation problems. Further, I had never faced anything quite so difficult before in my professional life. I wondered what I had gotten myself into.

But about this time, I received some good advice from some mentors to be forthright with my team about these problems. And so I did just that. I let everyone within the business school see the full report and all twenty-six key problems. I also let leadership across campus see what we were up against.

Similarly, I let our advisory board members and other key donors and supporters see the report and talked with them about the gravity of the problems. I basically confided in anyone I felt needed to know or whom I felt could help us be successfully reaccredited. That turned out to be the right thing to do. Everyone now knew exactly where we stood, and they saw the gravity of the problems we faced. Much to my surprise, nearly all of them leaned in and wanted to help.

As a leader in the higher education environment, you quickly discover the best way to get anything done is to do it *with* and *through* faculty. This is much like the president of the United States having to work with Congress or a corporate CEO needing to work with board members, top performers, and customers. With these monumental changes we had to make, I knew there was no way we were going to get any of them accomplished without the support and leadership of faculty members in the business school.

In addition to letting them all read the full report, I followed the advice of Bill and others and put together a task force of key faculty. This was led by Rick, the very well-respected professor in the finance program I mentioned earlier, and together, we dove into the accreditation report and made recommendations on how we could fix each of the twenty-six problems within the twelve-month deadline.

This wasn't a matter of delegating difficult problems to other people. Quite frankly, I needed the faculty's help to get this all done. On a side note, both Rick and Joe, one of my earlier amigos there, later joined me at my next institution, and both are still at that great institution and are very successful. My remaining third amigo, Mark, later moved on to be a successful dean and chancellor in his own right.

## SELF LESS LESSON:

### Transparency, Transparency, Transparency

The good news in being so transparent with everyone about reaccreditation was that everyone could see the same information at the same time. We all had the same sense of the problems we faced and the importance of working together to solve them. The bad news with being so transparent was that everyone in the business school was now acutely aware of the gravity of the situation and the difficulty in getting this all done on time.

Fortunately, I was able to persuade the accreditation agency to give us some extra time because I was new and a first-time dean. They graciously agreed to an additional six months, which provided a little more breathing room. Unfortunately, I now had a serious morale problem on my hands. Faculty members thought we were on the ropes and about to get knocked out. Thus, it was critical to convince people that immediate change was possible.

While having the extra six months helped shift people's attitudes, it still looked like a massive list of major changes that would challenge people's core values and assumptions about what type of business school this was and could become. We needed to quickly figure out how to first get people to believe this was all possible. We needed them to believe that we could accomplish our objective on time and that we would be a much better business school as a result.

Thank goodness, so many people stepped up to help me. One of these individuals was our management consultant, Bill, who was also one of the advisory board members. Bill loved the institution and cared deeply about our success. And for the next year and a half, he stepped in to provide me with invaluable counsel, becoming a close friend in the process.

At the point where I knew I had a *belief* problem, Bill provided some timely advice. He suggested I pull together a key group of leaders and influencers within the business school and hold a retreat at my house on the mountain near the campus. This would give us all a chance to get together in a personal setting, break bread together, and tackle this problem head-on.

I'll never forget the pivotal moment in this retreat. We gave all participants copies of one of the more popular, current rankings of the top 100 business schools around the country. That ranking measured business schools based on the perceptions of business school deans in terms of who they thought was the best. As such, this was a ranking largely based on a reputation survey, other peoples' perceptions of us, and our brand.

At the time, we were situated near the latter end of that ranking and in jeopardy of falling off the list completely if we were not successful in our reaccreditation bid. I was interested to see if the group would not only buy into the concept of reaccreditation but also be willing to dream. I invited them to imagine what it might be like to be seen as a top-ranked business school.

After our leadership team got a chance to digest the rankings and see that we were so far down the list, something magical happened. Several participants started to argue that we were being undervalued and that people had the wrong impressions of us and were downgrading us in that survey as a result. Other people commented that they had worked at business schools that were well ahead of us on the list, and these participants felt from personal experience that we were better than those schools.

That was when I had a rare stroke of genius. Based on what I was hearing, I asked everyone to take a moment and pull out their personal copy of the rankings. I then asked them to place one finger on our business school and move another finger up the list of schools, stopping only when they came to a school they believed was better than us.

After everyone was finished, I went around the room and asked each participant to call out which business school they selected and the number where that school was ranked. What happened next was remarkable.

With some four thousand colleges and universities of all types across the country, many of which included business schools, it was nice to be anywhere on the list of the top 100. We quickly went around the room to allow each of the twenty-five participants to weigh in. And to my surprise, each of them chose business schools that were ranked from twenty-fifth to thirty-fifth in the country. Think about that for a moment. Each of the participants believed we were on par with some of the best schools in the country and clearly believed we were much better than people around the country believed we were.

Next, I asked each of them to talk about why they chose the school they did and to explain how they believed we compared. The ensuing discussion was amazing. This exercise turned the entire tenor of the retreat into a conversation that was more about our strengths and why we were being overlooked rather than how bad we were. It was so powerful, so affirming, so forward looking, and so constructive.

Many of the participants even expressed anger that we weren't given a higher ranking. One department head practically shouted something to the effect of, "This AACSB stuff is a wake-up call. And we need to get this place shored up and get the damn word out about how good we are!"

You could sense the fear and disbelief fade as the ice thawed on our cultural organization. It was as though you could see the "unfreezing" that Kurt Lewin has written and spoken about so eloquently regarding successful organizational change. In that session, we not only unfroze the old culture and limiting beliefs that shackled us, but we also saw the possibilities ahead. It felt amazing, and I was so proud of that team and the breakthrough we experienced together.

That said, it's not as if this retreat solved all our problems. We talked a lot afterward about what we needed to do to fix everything the accreditation team wanted changed. Armed with a newfound sense of optimism and urgency, our spirits were high. That dovetailed nicely with the recommendations from the faculty task force, which provided a blueprint and buy-in from faculty about how to get everything fixed.

The rankings exercise and subsequent discussion enabled us to cross an all-important threshold from a place of limiting beliefs to a belief in the possible. We realized that what lay ahead of us could be accomplished. Caught up in this momentum, we went even further, not only charting a course for how to get through the reaccreditation bid but also charting a pathway toward being a top 25 business school among those at public universities like us. Our shifting beliefs were enabling a new value around the pursuit of excellence.

I'm proud to say that we got everything fixed and were successfully reaccredited within the eighteen-month time frame. And after this process was over, we kept going. We worked aggressively every day to continuously make the business school better at a time when many undergraduate business programs were stagnant or in decline.

We saw the future, and we jumped on it, with the team eventually launching an online MBA program to go along with online undergraduate programs we had already launched. Some years later, with one of my friends and teammates, Eric, at the helm, that program went on to be ranked as the number 1 online MBA program in the country, public or private. I'm proud of the work we put in together to get there, and I believe that getting over that hump with our limiting beliefs was the single-most difficult problem we faced.

## SELF LESS LESSON:

### It All Begins with the Belief That It Is Possible.

Allow me to share a fun aside from this accreditation experience that underscores the power of strong relationships. Two of the architects of the changes in that business school became lifelong friends. One was Eric, who was my associate dean, and he went on to successfully fill my spot as dean after I left. He then became dean at another excellent business school, at the University of California–Irvine, and did a great job there as well. Eric has remained a dear friend and mentor.

The second fellow, Dave, went on to be dean at Wyoming and did a great job there. Eventually, I was able to recruit him to be dean of the storied Drucker School of Management here at CGU, my current institution, and we are lucky to have him with us.

Also, on the theme of building great teams and developing strong, lasting relationships, I had the good fortune of helping assemble an incredibly diverse and talented leadership corps at UNLV, the big, urban university I led. Sometime after I left, that leadership team was ranked in an article in *Inside Higher Education* as being the most diverse among any university in the country (as measured by women and people of color in top leadership positions and among the best compensated at their university).

That experience forged strong relationships with two of the women who helped me build out that team, Diane and Nancy. Both played pivotal roles in the success we had and deserve much of the credit. Diane served with me for a time as a key vice president at my current institution, CGU, and has since moved on to be provost at Houston, a top-flight, public, R1 research university. Nancy still works back at UNLV in an endowed professorship and now serves on the Board of Trustees for us here at CGU.

## SELF LESS LESSON:

## Relationships Matter Not Only in the Moment but Down the Road As Well.

Another experience I had while in leadership roles at WSU shook my own beliefs to the very core. This one happened while I was running their foundation. Because I had helped spark a significant turnaround in giving, in addition to earlier leading a revival at the business school, I was told that I was being talked about as a possible candidate to succeed my boss as president. Then came a short but pivotal conversation after a university event in Seattle with a woman who was in a senior, key, external advisory role for the university.

She confirmed that, in fact, the regents had talked about me as a possibility for president, but in case I heard it from others, she wanted me to know that she had spoken against me because she felt I was *too nice to be a university president.*

I was speechless. I politely thanked her for being so candid, but as I walked away and processed what she had said, I shook my head and laughed. After I was safely out of earshot, I whispered quietly to myself, nodding my head, *I'm going to prove you wrong. I am going to Prove. You. Wrong.*

Clearly, she didn't believe in me. I respected her opinion, but by that point, I had developed a strong sense of myself and what I could do. Her lack of belief in me didn't shake my belief in myself. Further, my values about what I was doing were so strong and deep by that point that I wasn't going to let her limiting beliefs about me deter me from my path.

## SELF LESS LESSON:

### The Naysayers Never Go Away; They Just Have Fancier Titles.

Despite some naysayers like that along the way, I've been fortunate to be a part of many transformations, and overcoming limiting beliefs was a difficult problem in every case. Another situation that stands out took place during my first presidency at UNLV.

We were focused on becoming a Carnegie R1 research university—a stretch goal—so we selected good benchmarks in Arizona State University, the University of Houston, and the University of Central Florida. Each of these schools was much like us: large, urban, beautifully diverse, and embedded within and in service to a dynamic city. Unlike us, however, they had already reached the promised land: they were already Carnegie R1s and had accomplished so much more.

So, we sent teams from our university to visit these schools to see what was possible. As it turned out, the lessons we learned were instrumental in our success. More to the point, these other universities showed us there was a path forward. Becoming an R1 suddenly seemed possible.

This experience taught me there is perhaps no better shortcut than to learn and gain confidence from others who have already arrived at your destination.

**SO, I ASK YOU,** what might your limiting beliefs be about what is possible or not possible? More to the point, what might your limiting beliefs be as a leader? What might be the limiting beliefs among your team members, and how might they be holding the team and your organization back in what you all might accomplish? What can you do to help your team see what is possible? How might these beliefs shape prevailing values, and how might core values be driving or hindering what people believe is possible or desired? When you envision a positive, possible future for you and the others on your team, how does that feel?

# ACT THREE:

# ADVERSITY

**HAVE YOU ENCOUNTERED** *opposition as you tried to move your team or organization forward?* Has that opposition been visible or opaque? Have you ever encountered opposition so negative, divisive, and corrupt that it threatened not only to derail the success of your efforts but also to disrupt your career and those around you? If so, how can you manage these adversaries and successfully move forward with your head held high?

There are several types of adversity you're likely to face when transforming an organization. Many of them are environmental and things outside the organization that are likely beyond your control. Examples might include a pandemic or an economic downturn.

But the type of adversity I'm talking about here is the internal kind. It's the kind of adversity primarily stemming from people who are not onboard with your proposed changes. Don't count out or ignore those in opposition. You'll encounter them often, and you'll need to deal with them one way or another.

I've encountered many people during organizational transformations who were clearly not onboard and didn't want to do anything to help us change. Perhaps more surprising is that I frequently encountered people who actively tried to sabotage our efforts to move the organization forward. They can be incredibly damaging to the effort, especially if they are in an influential position within the organization.

When I first encounter these people, I embrace them and try to learn why they are opposed to me and the proposed changes. It may well be a case where they are right, and I am wrong. If so, I try to incorporate their thinking into the transformation and enable them to be a key architect in the change. If not, I try to change their mind. If that isn't possible, then I must work to manage around their opposition.

I've had many situations where a key influencer opposed what we were trying to do for all the wrong reasons and worked to undermine our efforts. Sadly, it happens at least once in nearly every transformation. Their efforts at sabotage might be nothing more than a private accusatory email to a key decision-maker, a negative comment whispered to a board member, or a confidential phone call to an important external supporter.

It's all passive-aggressive behavior and can be quite damaging. It forces the leader to undertake at least half a dozen corresponding calls, emails, or meetings to counteract the single action of the powerful naysayer. I don't want to focus too much on the negative people or negative actions, but it happens.

People like this are out there, and you'll have to manage through it. For significant organizational changes within large, complex organizations, I've even gone so far as to enlist a dedicated team and process to help us map out adversaries. I want to understand their opposition and manage the process of countering them.

## SELF LESS LESSON:

### Resistance Can Take Many Forms, Some Not Easy to See.

On the other hand, there were people whose opposition was more reasonable and subtle. We just couldn't convince them that we needed to change things or that the change was possible. They weren't sabotaging our efforts, but they had become immovable objects and were holding up progress. I recall the time I was recruited to go back to Arizona, to run the business school where I had earned my doctorate.

Among many planned changes, we needed to build and launch an online MBA program. On the heels of a great success with an online master's in information systems, a core group of faculty members were really excited about building the online MBA. However, a group of senior faculty members dug in their heels. They reasoned that the online information systems degree was fine, but MBA programs should be delivered in person because we were shaping leaders. And they argued that you couldn't accomplish this objective online.

That was a legitimate concern we needed to work through. With more conversation, we uncovered another key underlying reason for their reluctance: they not only felt that this modality didn't fit this type of *learning*, but they also didn't feel like it fit their style of *teaching*.

I explained till I was blue in the face how I had successfully built online MBA programs at two other universities and in one case for an MBA program at a much higher-ranked business school than ours. But to no avail. No amount of evidence or arguments would shift these faculty members' attitudes. Instead, we took a different tack. We were able to get them to agree to at least just sit on the sidelines on this one. We wouldn't expect them to do anything to help build, launch, or teach in the online MBA program. Instead, they could teach other courses in the on-ground MBA program and in other programs in more traditional modalities, which we needed, and they were good at.

We were successful in essentially getting this group of faculty members to politely stay out of the way of those who would pour their hearts into building and delivering a great online MBA. It's a good thing we did, because with enrollment declining in the traditional, on-ground MBA at that business school and across the country, we needed those online MBA enrollments to survive and thrive. We got to the place we needed to, but not with everyone onboard. Sometimes you must realize that you cannot get everyone's support, so you must either work around them or redirect them for other important tasks.

## SELF LESS LESSON:

### Sometimes You Need to Ask the Resistors to Step Aside.

One of the greatest things about being back at Arizona was that I got to work with so many talented, dedicated, fun people. A few of them were friends like Joe and Rick and others who came with me from our prior institution. Some were people I had been there with during my doctoral studies but hadn't gotten a chance to work with directly. Others were new friends like Jeff, Bob, Carol, and Barry. All were terrific, and it was one of the true honors in my life to be in service to my alma mater.

# One of the Toughest Challenges in My Life

I'd like to share another example of opposition that was pivotal for me both professionally and personally. While in my first presidency at UNLV, that dynamic, diverse, urban institution, I felt that we moved mountains to accomplish what we set out to do. It was an amazing time not just for that university but also for the community, business partners, the legislature, and the governor, all working together in the best interests of the university, the city, and the state.

We moved mountains and paved the way for the university to eventually achieve Carnegie R1 status, winning state funding for, and then launching and achieving preliminary accreditation for, a desperately needed new medical school. We also helped bring the NFL to town and found funding for the university football team to play in a new $2 billion stadium—all without the university having to pay for it directly.

In addition, we achieved Hispanic serving status and were ranked as the most diverse campus in the country. And we broke just about every record for that university, including enrollment, student success, fundraising, grants, and contracts, adding world-class academic and athletic facilities, creating many impactful corporate partnerships, and more. Working together, we accomplished a great deal in a short amount of time. This all sounds great, right?

Well, not so much.

Let's just say I had a tough time with the Board of Regents at that institution. This thirteen-member governing board was composed of elected officials representing districts around the state and was responsible for overseeing a multibillion-dollar higher ed enterprise including the two research universities, a smaller undergraduate-focused state college, a research institute, and four community colleges. That's a lot to oversee. Many of the elected board members at the time had never had the opportunity to be responsible for anything that large and complex.

I don't like to be negative, and I especially don't like to complain about people or cast them in a negative light. But suffice it to say there was a good deal of behavior among some of these regents that I did not condone, and it often put me in an untenable position.

Perhaps the most difficult thing to deal with was when they attacked my character and publicly tried to impugn my integrity in our quarterly board meetings. We had full media coverage at every meeting, and some regents would take advantage of the opportunity to "perform" for the cameras in the hopes of getting on the news that night or being mentioned in the morning papers. The media was always there, hoping for a regent's outburst, and they seldom came away disappointed.

Those who want to wade through the tawdry details can Google my name, and they'll find about twenty stories in the local newspapers around that time, mostly vindicating me and often outlining some of the questionable behavior on the part of some of those regents. At the time, this ordeal was among the hardest things I'd faced in my professional life. Some of these regents were trying to smear my name, push me out of the university, and destroy my career.

As someone who prides oneself on ethics, integrity, and personal morals, their attacks hit me hard. When I was in prior leadership roles at other universities, people tried to go after my integrity and character but never like this. Never at this level.

I learned a very good lesson from that painful process. In life, you want those whom you hold in high regard to have great respect for you. And you've got to try not to worry about the others. My incredible wife, Kristi, would console and support me through all of these trying times. In this instance, she told me something I'll never forget. She reminded me that this dynamic city in which we lived held 2.2 million inhabitants who loved me and supported me and that there were only four or five people in the state who wanted to get rid of me. I laughed and replied that I knew that, but the trouble was that those four or five people were among my board members and, in effect, were my bosses. We both got a good laugh out of that, and with much work, we were eventually able to put it all in perspective.

In terms of the organization and the progress, I was constantly having to move pieces around a figurative chessboard to outmaneuver this handful of regents. It caused a lot of overhead and extra time-consuming steps to get anything done. At times, I felt like a quarterback who had to contend with not only the eleven opposing players on defense but also players on my own team. This kind of thing forces you to be clever and creative and to do your best to laugh off foolish behaviors from petty people.

One illustrative example that sticks out happened in the early days of the stadium deal. With the help of some influential people in local industry, we invited an NFL owner to campus to discuss the possibility of working together in building a stadium. Some of the regents were demanding that I tell them where and when the meeting was taking place. I wanted them there, but I knew that if I told them with too much lead time where and when the meeting was going to be, they would leak it to the media, who would then be all over the meeting.

I stalled as much as I could, not telling them the exact location and specific meeting time until the last minute. We actually saw the media darting about town and campus trying to find the meeting. In the end, it went off without a hitch, and we managed to get these specific regents to arrive just in time as planned, and the media never did figure out where we were. My team and I were relieved that we were successful in our little gambit of maneuvering and misdirection.

On a more serious note, this all caused me to learn a lot about corporate governance. I saw what models worked and which ones didn't. And I learned what it meant to be a proper fiduciary and what happens when board members aren't. I also learned how a good board can propel an organization forward, while a few problematic board members can hold everyone back. Today, I could put on a master class in corporate governance for a university, though it might cause me to relive some painful moments.

More important, I learned useful lessons in patience and resilience. I was playing the long game and worked hard not to let those few adversaries hold me or the university back. I had to be resilient every day. When I got knocked down by these few adversaries, I rose up, dusted myself off, and got back in the game to make another play. In public meetings, while they hammered away at my character, I focused on staying the course. Like a Marine preparing for combat, I looked straight ahead, never showing any emotion, taking the hits, and responding calmly to pressure.

# SELF LESS LESSON:

## You'll Need to Develop Patience, Resilience, and Nerves of Steel.

I also had to be very careful to take care of myself physically, mentally, emotionally, and spiritually through those trying times.

Borrowing from techniques I learned from Tony Robbins, my wife, and others, I followed a helpful routine every morning. I started off with exercise, and then I would go out to the living room on a yoga mat and do some light stretching. As I stretched, I would get myself into a mindful and meditative state, and I go through a three-part *GAS routine.*

*Part one was the "G" for being grateful.* I would think about what I was grateful for in my life—including the love, health, and happiness of family members and close friends. I expressed gratitude for my good job, the good work that we were doing, the dynamic city we live in, and the nice home we have.

*Part two was the "A" for asking for help.* I would ask the universe to help ensure that my loved ones continued to be healthy, safe, happy, and fulfilled and that our efforts at the university would continue successfully. I would imagine that happening, and I would think about how good that would make me feel.

*Part three was the "S" for setting my intentions for the day.* I would think about what I set out to accomplish that day and how I would strive to seize the day and make it great. It took me only a few moments each morning, and it was a big part of my success in dealing with adversity and keeping my bearings.

As I reflect on that trying time, I'm reminded of John F. Kennedy's famous speech at Rice University in September 1962, shortly after I was born: "We choose to go to the Moon. We choose to go to the Moon in this decade and do the other things, not because they are easy, but because they are hard … because that challenge is one that we are willing to accept, one we are unwilling to postpone, and one which we intend to win."

That speech has consistently been lauded for the bold goal the president outlined for a lunar mission by the end of the decade. However, the element of the speech I keep coming back to is the sense that we do these important things not because they are easy, but because they are hard. Anything worth doing is going to be hard, filled with adversity, and have its share of naysayers along the way.

As Randy Pausch so beautifully described in his *The Last Lecture*, "The brick walls are not there to keep us out. The brick walls are there to show how badly we want something. Because the brick walls are there to stop people who don't want something badly enough. They are there to keep out the other people."

Life's most worthy pursuits are going to be blocked at every turn by obstacles and adversaries. So, buckle up buttercup, or as my fantastic high school football coach, Bob Owens, would bark at me, "Get your chinstrap on and get back out there!"

**SO HOW BAD DO YOU WANT IT?** Do you want to make a difference and have an impact? If so, are you ready to be tested in ways you cannot imagine? Are you ready to be stretched to the edge of your strength, endurance, patience, and resilience? And what can you be doing to better help yourself to weather these storms?

# ACT FOUR:

# IMPACT

**WHAT KIND OF** *impact do you want to have in your fleeting time on earth?* Would that impact be directed at other people or some other aspect of your lived experience? What might you change in your life now or in the coming days to better align with the impact and reputation you seek?

My life's purpose has gradually crystalized for me over the past several decades, and I've realized everything is all about impact. As I mentioned, when I get to the end of my path, I want to be able to look back and know in that moment that I did everything possible to have as much positive impact on as many people as I possibly could have and that I never shied away from an opportunity to do so.

When I initially crafted and then curated that purpose statement for myself over time, I thought very carefully about each word, each clause. You'll notice the ending clause, for example. I consciously put that last clause in the sentence about never shying away from an opportunity to serve others and have a positive impact on them. I've shared a lot about my sense of self and, in particular, my self-confidence.

I've felt that at times early on in my life, I shied away from saying or doing things or held back in my efforts toward something, because I lacked the confidence in myself in that moment. So, early on I vowed to myself I would not do this again. In the parlance of baseball, I wanted to "leave it all out on the field." Eventually, this notion made its way into my statement about my life's purpose.

I'm reminded of John Wayne's quote that "courage is being scared to death, but saddling up anyway." I realized at some point it was OK to have doubts and be nervous about attempting something outside my comfort zone. And I recognized fear had nothing to do with courage.

Courage is, as John Wayne so wryly pointed out, about finding the will to give it a try despite the fear. Once you realize that, you are free to own that fear and move ahead. I've felt like I subsequently had so many opportunities to stretch myself professionally, and I'm so proud I took those leaps of faith. After all, every sitting dean or president had to at some point be a first-time dean or a first-time president. I wasn't the only one.

## SELF LESS LESSON:

### Lighten Up on Yourself Because You're Not the First.

The other component of my purpose statement has to do with impact. In fact, impact is at the *core* of my purpose statement.

I want to have positive, visible, tangible, felt impact and not just a little. I want to have done as much of that as I possibly can. When I get to the end of this ride, I want to know I kept at it, didn't stop doing good, and didn't shy away from bigger opportunities that would enable me to impact more people in positive ways. I want to maximize that impact and, for the mathematicians out there, to do that asymptotically (i.e., tending toward infinity). Alternatively, for the layperson, just keep doing even more.

The final note about that purpose statement is that I am focused on positively impacting other people. In business, we often talk about having impact on people, profits, or planets, and the trade-offs for an organization between chasing after one of those versus another. There has been a lot of discussion about the difficulty in trying to maximize all three.

In my professional career, I have focused on maximizing my positive impact on people.

## SELF LESS LESSON:

### If You're Not Having Positive Impact on Others, What's the Point?

Why have I focused on impacting others? I'm not sure entirely why that is, but as I mentioned earlier, I suppose it probably has something to do with the impact my grandparents' sacrifices and immigration to America had on me. I learned so much from the subsequent lessons and values imparted to me by my parents, as well as the value I derived from higher education.

All of that shaped me as a person wanting to serve others and give back, channeled through a career in higher education. Now that I've had the opportunity to serve in leadership roles across several universities, I've also had an epiphany about why caring for and about others is so important to a leader.

Stop right here for a moment, clear your head, and think about this. What is the single greatest responsibility of any leader in just about any situation?

Here's my take. Think about all the time we spend at work. There are only twenty-four hours a day, and we spend about six to eight hours asleep. Next, consider those remaining waking hours you have each day. Think about the amount of time you spend working. Prior to the pandemic, it would have been typical to ask, "How much time do you spend *at work?*" Post-pandemic, with an increase in remote work, it might be better to ask, "How much time each day do you spend working?" In either case, we spend a big chunk of our waking hours working, typically a minimum of eight hours for most people. For many of us who continue to work at least part of the time remotely from home, it feels like we never stop working.

The remaining time each day is typically spent in a flurry of activities, such as working out, picking up kids, grocery shopping, running other errands, making dinner, making sure kids get their homework done, and getting kids to bed. We each typically have a brief frenzy of activity at the end of the day, right after work, and before we go to sleep. Correspondingly, we have that frenzy each morning getting up, getting ready, getting kids prepped and off to school, and getting ready to drive to work or preparing for a day in the home office.

The point I'm trying to make is that on a typical day, most people spend a significant portion of their waking hours working, getting ready for, or winding down from work, getting to and from work, taking calls and answering emails related to work, thinking about work, or worrying about work. You get the picture.

In our modern westernized society, work dominates our limited waking hours. So, if you think about it carefully, as a leader in an organization, the people under your charge are spending a disproportionately large proportion of their limited waking hours with you working. Given that people spend so much of their lives working, wouldn't you as the leader want to try as hard as you can to make sure this time is well spent? Wouldn't you want to make sure they are spending that time meaningfully?

And by meaningfully, I mean meaningfully to *them*, not necessarily to the organization. This means they need time that enables them to fulfill their purpose in life, time to do something constructive and productive, time from which they can derive some form of meaning in life. At a minimum, wouldn't you want people to at least have some fun while working, at least occasionally? To be at least occasionally happy at work, perhaps even to laugh out loud occasionally while working? Shouldn't that be important, given the time each person devotes to work?

If you look at any of the statistics or survey results around people's engagement at work, you will sadly surmise they generally aren't "feeling it" while they work. National stats on workplace engagement are abysmally low each year. Tom Peters reminded me recently that this low level of workplace engagement is, sadly, a global phenomenon. Collectively, we leaders aren't doing a very good job of making work meaningful for people, and what a sad waste of their time and their lives that is. What a missed opportunity for us as leaders to make a difference in people's lives.

Here at CGU and guided by the writings of the late Peter Drucker, namesake for our storied business school, I believe our obligation to society is to do everything within our authority to ensure the time people spend working is meaningful, has purpose, and brings them fulfillment and happiness.

Remember that we sit in these seats of leadership for a brief, fleeting moment, and it's a privilege not to be taken lightly. So be grateful, make the most of it, leave it better than you found it, let others have the credit, and make sure they are having fun and doing things that are meaningful to them.

In short, take care of others who are taking the ride with you.

## SELF LESS LESSON:

**As Leader Your Ultimate Responsibility Is to Others.**

As I mentioned earlier, we accomplished a lot during my time at UNLV, that incredible, diverse state university in that dynamic city out West.

Seeing the stadium, the medical school, Carnegie R1, and so many other projects and goals come to fruition leaves me with an intense feeling of pride, fulfillment, and happiness. When I look back on all that, however, I derive the most satisfaction and fulfillment from the small, relatively random acts of kindness we were able to engage in as we served others.

I think that perhaps the single greatest accomplishment from my time at that institution might be something that didn't get written about much in the newspapers. When I arrived at that institution, there was a generous personnel benefit available to faculty and the professional staff that essentially offered nearly free tuition and fees to that person's spouse and dependents. It was a heck of a deal!

My listening tour during my first hundred days on the job there spanned the campus, the community, parts of the state, and alumni around the country. As part of the tour, I met with groups of faculty and staff from nearly every unit on campus, literally thousands of people. While I might not have been able to have one-on-one conversations with everyone, I at least got to meet with them in small groups and hear their feedback.

In one of those meetings, I chatted with one of the grounds crew supervisors, Conrad. The grounds at that university are spectacular, and I thanked him for his work. That friendly conversation ultimately led to what I considered a good friendship between the two of us during my time there. One of the things that struck me during our initial meeting was that Conrad had the courage to speak up and let me know that a grave mistake was being made with respect to that tuition benefit. He was serious, and I was intrigued, so we agreed to discuss it further in private.

We later met, and he explained that the incredible tuition benefit available for faculty and professional staff was not extended to the classified staff. This included groundskeepers like Conrad, as well as people in areas such as maintenance, janitorial, secretarial, and bookkeeping—the people who needed that tuition benefit the most for their spouses and dependents. I quickly got it, and like him, I felt it was egregious that we were not extending this benefit to the classified staff.

Together, along with several others, we worked on solving this problem, and in the process, Conrad spoke out several times for this change during the public comment period in front of the regents. That took a lot of courage, given what I've shared about the rancor at these meetings. We got it done, but it took way more time than it should have to get this approved. Our campus was quick to come together on this policy change, but Conrad and I encountered way too much resistance from people at the system office and from other campuses around the state.

## SELF LESS LESSON:

### Sometimes What Seems to Be the Small Stuff Is Often the Most Important and Difficult.

In retrospect, I suspect that some of the other campuses didn't want us to get ahead of them with this new benefit before they could offer it too. I think that some folks in the system office might have also wanted to make sure other campuses weren't caught flat-footed on this initiative. We also had evidence that others wanted to take credit for implementing this new benefit, and so that also slowed everything down.

No matter. We didn't care who got the credit, and it was fine for other universities and colleges in the system to jump in on this initiative. We just wanted to see it get done. I'm reminded of the old Ronald Reagan adage that it is amazing what you can accomplish when you don't worry about who gets the credit.

In any event, we got this done, and I give the credit to Conrad. This change was and continues to be truly transformational in people's lives in perpetuity on that campus. Think about a janitor or groundskeeper or food server there now being able to send their child to college and how that transforms that family.

Being in service to people who needed it most is critical. That is your obligation—to have that kind of opportunity to serve others, to have that kind of impact, and to leave that kind of legacy.

**SO, I ASK YOU AGAIN,** what kind of impact do you want to have? And what are you doing about it in your life each day? Your time on this earth is brief in the grand scheme of things, and your time in the seat of leadership is such a fleeting privilege. Don't you want to make the most of it?

# ACT FIVE:

# LEGACY

**DO YOU EVER** *stop to think about how what you are doing and saying today is having an impact on others?* How do others perceive that impact now? And how will that lasting legacy continue to shape others after you're gone?

Perhaps one of the most surprisingly satisfying elements of my career in higher education has been fundraising. But it was not on my radar when I began my career. As a newly minted PhD graduate, embarking on a career as a business school professor, I was mostly focused on trying to stay ahead of my students in the classes I taught. My goal was to keep my research projects afloat amid demanding teaching assignments, to be a good and active citizen within my school and within the information systems professional association. That's a tall order for a junior faculty member!

I quickly figured out, however, that the university couldn't possibly fund the many great ideas I had for my program and for my own research. For example, my colleagues and I wanted to be able to teach in a fully automated, futuristic classroom setting. Similarly, we wanted to be able to conduct our research within a custom-designed, private research lab with all the needed bells and whistles. Not being one to take no for an answer, I set out to figure out how to secure funding to breathe life into these ideas and visions.

In doing so as a junior faculty member, I dove headfirst into the world of philanthropy without even knowing it, and what a terrific experience it was. Early on, I got to work with some amazing people and organizations external to my university as they helped fund futuristic classrooms and state-of-the-art research labs. I didn't think of it at the time as fundraising per se. Rather, I had some cool stuff I wanted to do. And then I found people with means with whom our cool ideas resonated, and I was able to work with others to persuade them to give us some money to help us build these cool facilities.

Fast-forward a few decades, and I've now had the privilege to help raise a lot of money. I've lost count, but if I try to add it all up, including related gifts-in-kind, such as software, hardware, land and buildings, and artwork, it's close to a billion dollars. There have been so many cool projects!

For example, I got to help build several "classrooms of the future" with tech companies and donors as partners. These facilities transformed learning for so many. Similarly, raising money to launch a medical school led to so much transformational impact for those students, for that university, for that community both socially and economically, and for the many lives to come that the medical school will serve.

## Raising Money on the Palouse

I learned so much through fundraising that I could tell stories over wine for hours on end. So many great people, so many great projects, so much tremendous impact, and so many valuable lessons learned. I recall, for example, when I first stepped in to lead the overall fundraising for WSU, that storied university on the beautiful inland Palouse area in the Pacific Northwest.

I was serving for Lane, a president who was a smart visionary. I'll never forget that as we embarked on our first fundraising trip together to some exotic place, Lane turned to me and said something like, "You know, Len, you and I are going to get to meet some amazing people and go to some unbelievable places, but never forget where you're from. And don't get too carried away by this fancy lifestyle that you and I are going to get to briefly experience together."

Lane and I both had humble upbringings, and he has turned out to be a great friend and mentor for me to this day. His words proved prophetic as he and I got to join some of our donors in unforgettable experiences at unbelievable destinations. And in the process, we helped that school raise a lot of money.

Up to that point, I had raised money as a faculty member, department chair, and dean, but I never had quite the same experiences in raising money prior to that job as the university's chief fundraising officer. We got to spend time with amazing people in fantastic homes, ranches, start-ups, corporate offices, planes, boats, country clubs, and so on. Even better, we got to visit troubled schools we were helping and spend time in desperate neighborhoods. On one trip, we visited a church in Birmingham, Alabama, famous for its role in the civil rights movement.

One experience on that trip to Alabama involved a simple gesture from a donor that stands out because it showed how much she cared about us. She was the widow of an alum, and she had asked us to go with her to a special football game between our university (her late husband's alma mater) and her alma mater in another city.

It meant so much to her that we were experiencing that game with her that she had two custom cakes made. One had the logo of our university, and the other had the logo of her alma mater. It was a very simple gesture on her part yet so thoughtful and caring. What an amazing person she was, and what an unforgettable experience.

Throughout this narrative, I've mentioned the many mentors who helped me on my journey, much like Lane at WSU. They've played a huge role in my life. Right from the beginning I've always openly, actively sought out help, and I can think of very few cases where anyone turned me down. In fact, in many cases the help has evolved into an ongoing, formal mentorship kind of relationship.

Even today, I benefit from the wise counsel of many university presidents, board members, business leaders, elected officials, consultants, and others. And these experiences taught me a valuable life lesson. You're never too old, successful, experienced, or smart to benefit from the mentoring of someone else. For any success I've had it is most likely attributable to mentoring from someone, particularly on the fundraising side of the university.

## SELF LESS LESSON:

### You're Never Too Old to Need a Mentor.

Some of the other lessons learned in fundraising struck me because they so closely paralleled what I learned and loved about my time as an athlete.

Fundraising is, inherently, a contact sport. Contact sports include football and basketball, as well as contemporary sports like mixed martial arts. These are sports, unlike baseball, in which athletes come into direct physical contact with one another often throughout the game. You can't tell if the sweat and occasional blood on your uniform is yours or your opponents. Not that fundraising involves that kind of contact, but success in fundraising lies in direct, deep, frequent contact with your donors. It's a relationship-based endeavor, to say the least.

Many of the most significant gifts I had the opportunity to be involved in were based on substantial relationships with the donor and their family. Many of them continue to be close friends, and I know them, their families, their business ventures, their politics, and so on quite extensively. I recall one donor, Scott, the leader of a major aircraft manufacturing company, who credited his success to his business degree at the university at which I worked, WSU.

His philanthropy and business success increased steadily as our relationship grew. For one of many major gifts from him, we had him and his family over to our house out in the country on the mountain, the "mountain house" I referenced in the Prologue. That day stands out not only because of the huge bull moose that showed up as if on cue for our guests but also because of the closeness I felt with him.

Therein lies the second athletics-themed lesson I learned about fundraising. It is not only a *contact* sport but also a *team* sport. It takes people from throughout the university to interact with even just one donor—a team that typically includes a major gift officer, a dean, the vice president of development, the president, the alumni association director, and perhaps the athletics director, a coach, a professor the donor once had for class, a staff member who was helpful, and others, all working in a coordinated fashion to properly cultivate that donor over a lifetime and curate a memorable experience.

# SELF LESS LESSON:

## Relationship Building Is a Contact and Team Sport, and There Is No "I" in Team.

Even more to the point, however, I realized that for many donors like Scott, the relationship with the university began long ago. It carried through his experience as a student and well beyond, perhaps for decades, before I had even met him.

I had the opportunity to sit briefly in the seat as dean and later as vice president of development. I was, in effect, a fleeting interloper in a donor's lifelong love affair with the university. I was not the driver of that person's giving. Rather, his lifelong love of the university was the driver. I just had the privilege of sharing in it with him for a brief time.

Toward that end, a very wise fundraising consultant, Bruce, once told me that fundraising brought him so much happiness and fulfillment. He then encouraged me to stop for a minute and chose three of four of those moments in my life that were truly special. After pausing for a moment to collect my thoughts, I told him it would be the birth of each of my children and maybe graduating with my PhD.

Bruce then replied by pointing out that donors are no different from me. They too have three or four moments in their lives much like mine that really mean something to them. I asked if that meant I needed to learn what these moments were so that I could truly get to know them. Bruce laughed and said that would be great if I was lucky enough to know these donors in this way, but that I'd missed the point of his lesson.

I asked him to please explain, and he said that the donors are choosing to give philanthropically of their wealth and have great impact on others. They are lucky in that they can leave a legacy with their giving. In fact, for many of them, no matter whether their gifts are large or small, they will include in their mind their gift(s) among their most special moments in life, along with the birth of their children or earning that degree or getting that big promotion at work.

He went on to say that what he loved most about fundraising was that it gave him the opportunity to participate in some incredibly special philanthropic moments in people's lives. He was privileged to share in that special moment as they did something loving and giving for someone else. And the longer Bruce spoke, the more he helped me realize why I love fundraising so much. I'll never forget his wise lesson, and I think I've appreciated fundraising even more ever since.

## SELF LESS LESSON:

### Leadership Is Often a Gift and Privilege in Being Allowed to Experience Moments with Others When They Are at Their Best.

Bruce imparted another practical lesson to me that also proved useful, especially as I moved into university presidencies.

He drew a picture for me that he said would remind me of the old Mastercard logo. You'll recall that logo with the "Mastercard Red" circle on the left and the "Mastercard Yellow" circle on the right, and they converge a bit in the middle like a Venn diagram, with the two circles intercepting and overlapping each other.

Bruce then explained that the circle on the left represented things I wanted to do for the university that required funding, like the classroom of the future projects back when I was a professor, or more recently the medical school we were trying to launch. He further explained that the circle on the right represented things that the donors wanted the university to do and that the donor was willing to pay for. I could then see where he was going and wondered how he would describe the overlap.

Anticipating my question, Bruce smiled and said, "The middle is where the magic happens." He explained that the items in the circle on the left were ideas, visions, and projects I thought were important but were different from my donors' desires. And no amount of effort would convince them otherwise. In fact, he argued, I shouldn't try to force donors into those projects if they didn't want them, because in the end, those donors wouldn't be happy with their investment.

For the circle on the right, Bruce argued, it would include many neat ideas the donor wanted the university to do but were things I should not pursue just because I wanted to "land the gift." He said that if, in fact, I chased after those types of gifts and got them, those projects would not be important to the university and, as such, would take a back seat. And ultimately, those donors would not be happy with how their investment was being treated. This was very wise advice!

Bruce went on to explain that when I found people who really liked what we had determined were the university's most vital needs and most impactful projects, where in a sense my own values and vision for advancing the university resonated on a deep and consistent level with the donor's own values and vision, *that* was where the magic would happen. That was the overlap in the middle. He added that, perhaps even better yet, I might find situations where I would co-create with the donor that future for the university. That was where and when I would find true success in fundraising, and that was where and when we would truly advance the institution.

I was able to then participate in some truly transformational gifts that were also incredibly meaningful to the donors. More than a few tears of happiness were shed in the process of cultivating, implementing, and stewarding those gifts. And when the tears appear, you know that you and your team, as well as the donors and their families and advisors, are working on something meaningful, impactful, rare, and special.

## SELF LESS LESSON:

### Beautiful Things Can Happen When Values Align.

Bruce's Mastercard diagram lesson, his encouragement to participate in special moments with donors, and my lessons learned about fundraising being a contact and team sport were a powerful combination. Combining these three lessons with other tips I learned along the way shaped my fundraising in many healthy and productive ways. It also saved me from having a destructive mindset.

For example, I never subscribed to the "own a donor" mentality that is prevalent on a lot of university campuses. I didn't believe the athletics department or business school should own their own donors and not want anyone else talking to that person. We don't own our donors. With a donor-centric approach, we're there for *them*. We're trying to help them achieve special, unforgettable moments of philanthropy with tremendous impact. It doesn't matter where within the university that gift is aimed, as long as it advances the institution in a meaningful way. And it doesn't matter who gets the credit.

Over decades of fundraising in higher education, I've had many funny or awkward moments that stand out. When Scott, that executive I mentioned earlier, made one of his first large gifts to the university to help us to build a career center for our business students, he initially wanted to name the facility after me. I was flattered, but I explained to him that we needed to name that facility after his family. It was their legacy, not mine. So, we named it after his family, and after many more large gifts to that business school, along with a significant estate commitment, that business school now proudly carries his family's name.

In a similar situation during my first presidency, I went to bat for the new medical school we were launching when it appeared that state funding for operations would be cut back significantly. Out of desperation, and against the wishes of my board and system head, I traveled to the state capitol with my governmental relations director and met personally with the governor to plead with him to restore the full funding that had been promised.

And thankfully, we were able to work with him and the legislative leaders to get it all back. This was no small feat. As a result, donors who then committed nearly $200 million in funding for the facilities needed for the medical school joked that they wanted to name the main building after me. Cooler heads prevailed, and that building, now complete, carries the name of the family from which a good portion of the funding comes, a family name that means a lot to that city and its growth and evolution. Again, this was more appropriate to that family's legacy than mine and indeed to the legacy of that city.

# SELF LESS LESSON:

## Sometimes It Is More about Their Legacy and Less about Yours.

I've had countless meaningful situations along the way, but the most remarkable are those tearful moments of pure personal goodness on the part of the donors, participating with them in their moment of philanthropy when they made that decision to give. Those moments stand out.

One I especially remember didn't involve an actual gift, but rather, a very special moment of stewardship long after this particular donor had done his giving, had his impact, and ensured his legacy. It happened on a golf cart ride.

While at UNLV, I had established a vast network of relationships throughout the community. One day I received a call from Randy, one of our university foundation board of trustee members. That trustee was and is a very successful and well-respected wealth manager in the region, and he and his wife had become good friends with me and my wife. The call was quick, as my calls with him often were, and incredibly helpful, as they always were.

Randy confidentially told me that a longtime donor to the university, Irwin, was not in good health and would soon be passing. This donor had been part of a small group of influential commercial real estate developers in that city who cobbled together the acreage needed way back when for the fledgling university. And together, they'd donated hundreds of prime acres that the university's main campus now sits on.

Irwin was later involved in the construction of many of the buildings on campus, in addition to other significant gifts to the university along the way. The trustee on that call suggested I take Irwin for a golf cart ride around the campus, kind of a nice trip down memory lane. Our trustee hoped that the ride would bring Irwin some satisfaction and comfort in his final days.

I quickly grabbed our vice president of development, Scott, and we scheduled a visit for Irwin within a few days. He arrived with his wife in the special-access van that transported him and his wheelchair. His driver and his wife carefully got Irwin out of the van and into the golf cart. The vice president drove so that Irwin, his wife, and I could focus on the tour.

Irwin didn't say much as we rode along, with the vice president and I reminding him along the way of the time he and his colleagues brought all that land together for the university. As we drove by buildings he had helped build, we talked about programs and students who had flourished as a result. We were also careful to draw out the subsequent role that all of it played in enabling more recent projects like the new stadium and medical school. Irwin couldn't communicate too well, but he frequently fought back tears throughout that ride. His occasional, brief comments and questions, among stifled bursts of pure emotion, let us know that the ride meant a lot to him. It also confirmed that our trustee's instincts were spot-on about what we needed to do for Irwin that day.

We helped his wife and driver get him ensconced safely back in the van, and his wife thanked us profusely. It was evident the ride meant a lot to them. I'm not sure why it came to me in that moment, but I felt I needed to say something. As I stood outside the van, reaching in and shaking his hand, I asked Irwin if he had ever heard the famous quote attributed to Isaac Newton, "standing on the shoulders of giants." He shook his head, indicating that he hadn't. It is reported to be something that Newton wrote in a letter to fellow mathematician Robert Hooke, though it is thought that Newton wasn't the first to say it. In any event, the quote goes something like this: "If I have seen further, it is by standing on the shoulders of giants."

I walked through the quote for him, and I emphasized those last few words as my voice broke and I began to get emotional. I explained that all these tremendous things we were doing at the university, and all the subsequent impact that we were having on people's lives, all flowed from the work that Irwin and his colleagues did for us with their grant of all that land to the university. By then we were all crying—Irwin, me, his wife, our vice president. Even Irwin's driver appeared moved. It was a moment of stewardship, of thanks, of affirmation for Irwin of the impact he had and of his legacy. It was a moment I will never forget.

## SELF LESS LESSON:

### There Is Perhaps Nothing Better Than Helping Secure the Legacy of Someone Else.

Special moments like that one with Irwin have inspired me to think a lot about my own life, from my origins and heritage to how I've lived my life through my drive, efforts, relationships, and integrity. I've thought about how people perceive me in terms of their level of respect for me and my reputation as shaped by their perceptions of me. This includes my own ongoing assessment of my impact. Lately, I've been thinking more and more about my legacy and how I'll be remembered long after I'm gone.

As the old saying goes, you die twice—the first time when your physical life force finally leaves your body and the second time upon the passing of the last person on earth who has a direct memory of you. Of course, your reputation can live on with your name, image, likeness, and writings about you surviving in print or digital form. Your legacy, however, lives on in terms of the continued impact your efforts and investments have on successive generations long after you're gone.

While your name might not necessarily be tangibly associated with these long-lasting efforts, the impact is there, nonetheless. That impact continues to breathe life into your legacy, one successive life at a time. It may be without fanfare, but the effect is real, and it stems from you.

I'll remind you of my life's purpose again: *When I get to the end of my path, I want to be able to look back in that moment and know that I did everything I possibly could, to positively impact as many people as I possibly could, and that I never shied away from an opportunity to do so.*

I feel that I am doing nearly everything I possibly can to maximize that positive impact. Some days are better than others, but the important thing is that I keep trying to do all I can. My sense of this is that it is within my power to maximize my effort and to try to maximize the impact. While I won't be there to shape my legacy, I'm paying into that account now in the belief that it will pay dividends down the road. Other people will determine later what my legacy is. If I do everything I can now, I'm willing to let the chips fall where they may.

After I'm gone, I think the highest praise people could give me would be to say I was a nice guy who worked hard. That I never lost my sense of myself. That I stayed within myself, in a sense. I would also hope people would say, borrowing from the lyrics of Tim

McGraw, that I was nearly always humble and kind. That would be something that would make both my mom and my dad happy, and so that's good enough for me.

In fact, I cringe when I hear or read someone trying to say that I am a good leader. I think that leadership is a "work in process," a state you never achieve. I feel that leadership is, in some weird Zen kind of way, a state of being you work to achieve but perhaps never actually arrive at, and that's OK.

Leadership is perhaps better thought of as trying to reach a state of true enlightenment. It's about the pursuit and not the destination. I don't think of myself less as a leader per se. Rather, I think of myself more as being a *student* of leadership, always learning and growing, always trying to get better at the craft, and always trying to learn from others and to do good for others as a result.

The other important lesson I've learned about leadership is that there is no one best way to lead. And there is no one best leadership style or approach. In fact, as do Hersey, Blanchard, and others, I believe that on some fundamental level, leadership is highly situational. My approach in one organization didn't necessarily mirror my approach in another organization. In every situation, I needed to change my approach. And in some cases, I had to shift my approach for different situations within the same organization.

My enduring values and core personality didn't change. Rather, my approach with people changed. I also realized that, despite the admonition of that regent some years ago, it wasn't in fact the case that I was "too nice to be a university president." That was far from the truth. I think that being nice was not only my natural state of being, but that it was also critical to whatever successes we've had.

# SELF LESS LESSON:

## Leadership Is an Ongoing and Endless Pursuit, Process, and Journey. It Is Not a Definitive Outcome, Destination, or Fixed Trait.

I hope that I have many good years ahead. In the words of Robert Frost, I have miles to go before I sleep. I'm sixty-two years old as I tell this story, and my dad passed early at sixty-five. I'm taking better care of myself now than my dad did then, and I also benefit from better nutrition and healthcare. In any event, I hope and expect that there is still a lot of open road ahead of me as well as continued opportunities to have an impact.

As I look back on my life, I'm not sure I've done enough yet to have paid back my ancestors for the sacrifices they made or to even make my mom and dad proud of the totality of my efforts on balance—the good and the bad. That's why I aim to keep pushing hard for as long as I can so that in the end I'll feel that I left it all out on the field.

On the one hand, I'm at this point a two-time business school dean and a two-time university president. I've had a lot of opportunities to have deep impact. On the other hand, in many ways, I'm still that quirky Italian squirt, the son of a fireman, the grandson of Italian immigrants, still unsure, still working on my confidence, continuing to want to learn and grow and to be in service to others.

The good news is that I'm still surrounded by a lot of incredible people at work from whom I learn every day, and I also continue to be surrounded by loving, talented, supportive people in my family and friends. To the extent that I've had any impact, it is because of their love and support.

To those of you who have kept reading to the end, I want to thank you for your patience and for the generous amount of free time you apparently have on your hands. Thanks for listening to my story. Thanks for taking the time to learn about someone else. I hope this caused you to think about your own life and legacy and the impact you have on others. If you have, thanks for that as well. Whatever your pursuits, I wish you well. And I hope that part of my legacy might be to cause you to think a bit more about your own.

**THE FINAL QUESTION** I'll leave you with is this: *Do you ever think about the impact you're having, and whether there might be continuing impact from your efforts after you're gone?* What might your legacy be as a result of your efforts and impact, and how might people perceive it and you long after you're gone? Are you doing all you can now to shape that impact and legacy in ways that enable you to continue to do good even when you're not here to do it yourself?

# EPILOGUE

**I TRIED TO** focus on the positive, but please understand that this all didn't come without sacrifice, pain, sadness, and regrets. I've experienced all of that along the way, and I've certainly made mistakes. Many were relatively small, but some were big. There are some things I wish I would have handled differently, and in those cases, I tried hard to learn from those mistakes.

I look back, for example, and I think that my drive and focus about my life's purpose as it instantiated in my professional life probably had something to do with the breakup of my first marriage. I learned from that, and I feel that I'm doing a better job in my second marriage. I also moved out of town to pursue a bigger leadership opportunity at another university, but I moved at a point when my son and daughter were still at tender ages and needed to stay behind with their mom.

I continued to support my kids financially, talked and did video calls with them frequently, and flew back to see them for weekends every three or four weeks throughout the year. They also visited me on extended stays for holidays and in summer. Even as they grew older, we continued to fly back and forth to spend time with each other for many years along the way. They have now reached college age, one pursing an undergrad degree and the other having just completed her master's degree.

It wasn't optimal for them when I left, and I know it was even more difficult for them than it was for me. I vividly recall the conversation I had with them when I first left to take a job in another state. I explained to them, fighting back tears, that I needed to take this other job and that I wanted to make sure they would be OK with that. My kids basically said, "Dad, you got this. We'll be fine. Go for it!" They reminded me in that moment that they were likely smarter than I would ever be and that I would have to continue to work hard to live up to their perceptions of the person they felt I was and am.

My meta-level lesson from all of this is that I work hard to continue to learn and, in some cases, continue to learn how to learn. I continue to learn and grow in being a better dad, friend, brother, husband, partner, and leader. I've focused on being caring, loving, supportive, respectful, kind, and in service to others. This includes being both selfless as a state of mind and self less as a state of action. Selfless leadership isn't about arriving at a specific destination. It's a habitual choice leaders must make every day.

I think that now for me it is also about continuing to be a student of leadership and of life. I want to continue learning, to grow with voracious curiosity, and to be excited for what may come next. I'm truly grateful for the opportunity each day to be enlightened. I suppose you could say that I devoted my life not only to being in service to others but also to learning. Learning has certainly played a profound role in my life, and it continues to do so.

Indeed, I can't wait to see what lessons tomorrow brings.

# ACKNOWLEDGMENTS

**SO MANY PEOPLE** have helped me along the way, including friends, teachers, professors, coaches, classmates, colleagues, team members, mentors, business partners, board members, donors, and more. Several of them are described in this story, and there are too many to list here. I sincerely thank them all for their support and belief in me. This story would be quite different if not for their wise counsel and assistance.

Sincere thanks to several friends, family members, and colleagues who read earlier versions of this story and gave very helpful comments. In particular, I want to thank a few fantastic colleagues, including Tim Lynch, Ezra Byer, and Jennifer Villalobos, who gave this a lot of time and effort. Their editing and developmental feedback were invaluable.

I would like to offer a special callout to my family, going all the way back to my ancestors, for their love, support, and sacrifices that enabled and fueled me and made this story possible. I thank, especially, my loving wife, Kristi, who had more to do with this story both in its unfolding and its telling than I think she realizes. She rivals my mom as one of the most loving, caring, and nicest people on the planet, beautiful on the inside and out.

Finally, I want to thank my two incredible kids—Jamie, my daughter, and David, my son. I continue to be so proud of them both and love them both so much. In words paraphrased from a very special Zac Brown lyric, I hope that in my seemingly single-minded pursuit of my purpose, they didn't mistake me for a father who didn't care at all.

# BIBLIOGRAPHY

## PROLOGUE

Blackburn, Robert T., and Janet H. Lawrence. *Faculty at Work: Motivation, Expectation, Satisfaction.* Baltimore: Johns Hopkins University Press, 1995.

Bligh, Michelle C., Craig L. Pearce, and Jeffrey C. Kohles. "The Importance of Self and Shared Leadership in Team Based Knowledge Work: A Meso-Level Model of Leadership Dynamics." *Journal of Managerial Psychology* 21 (2006): 296–318.

Bunting, Joe. "Five Act Structure: Definition, Origin, Examples, and Whether You Should Use It in Your Writing." The Write Practice. Accessed September 12, 2023. https://thewritepractice.com/five-act-structure/.

Chiu, Chia-Yen Chad, Bradley P. Owens, and Paul E. Tesluk. "Initiating and Utilizing Shared Leadership in Teams: The Role of Leader Humility, Team Proactive Personality, and Team Performance Capability." *Journal of Applied Psychology* 101 (2016): 1705–1720.

Coldplay. "Fix You Lyrics." Genius. Accessed September 12, 2023. https://genius.com/Coldplay-fix-you-lyrics.

Collins, Jim. "Level 5 Leadership: The Triumph of Humility and Fierce Resolve." *Harvard Business Review* 83, no. 7 (2005): 136.

Collins, James C. *Good to Great: Why Some Companies Make the Leap and Others Don't.* New York: Harper Business, 2001.

Day, Liza, and John Maltby. "Forgiveness and Social Loneliness." *The Journal of Psychology* 139, no. 6 (2005): 553–555. DOI: 10.3200/ JRLP.139.6.553.

Joubert, Stephan. "A Well-Played Life: Discernment as the Constitutive Building Block of Selfless Leadership." In *Leading in a VUCA World: Integrating Leadership, Discernment and Spirituality,* edited by Jacobus (Kobus) Kok, Steven C. van den Heuvel, 139–150. New York: Springer, 2019.

Kissinger, Henry. *Leadership: Six Studies in World Strategy.* New York: Penguin Press, 2022.

Kotter, John P. "What Leaders Really Do." *The Bottom Line* 13, no. 1. (2000). https://doi.org/10.1108/bl.2000.17013aae.001.

Lowery, Brian. *Selfless: The Social Creation of You.* New York: HarperCollins Publisher, 2023.

Maxwell, Richard, and Robert Dickman. "Changing Our Organizations through the Power of Story." The Systems Thinker. 2018. https://thesystemsthinker.com/ changing-our-organizations-through-the-power-of-story/

Noble, Linda M. "Mentoring from Your Department Chair: Building a Valuable Relationship." In *Handbook of the Teaching of Psychology,* edited by William Buskist, Stephen F. Davis, 328–332. 2006.

Oudheusden, Katrijn Van. *Selfless Leadership: A Complete Guide to Awakening the Servant Leader Within.* 2022.

Peters, Thomas J. *Excellence Now: Extreme Humanism.* Chicago: Networlding Publishing, 2021.

Peters, Thomas J., and Nancy Austin. *A Passion for Excellence: The Leadership Difference*. New York: Random House, 1985.

Peters, Thomas J., and Robert H. Waterman. *In Search of Excellence: Lessons from America's Best-Run Companies*. New York: Harper & Row, 1982.

Popper, Micha, and Ofra Mayseless. "The Building Blocks of Leader Development: A Psychological Conceptual Framework." *Leadership & Organization Development Journal* 28, no. 7 (2007): 664–684.

Reis, Harry T., and Shelly L. Gable. "Toward a Positive Psychology of Relationships." In *Flourishing: Positive Psychology and the Life Well-Lived*, edited by Corey L. M. Keyes and Jonathan Haidt, 129–159. American Psychological Association, 2003.

Roberts, David. "Lessons Learned from Selfless Leadership." *Forbes*, May 23, 2023. Accessed September 12, 2023. https://www.forbes.com/sites/forbestechcouncil/2023/05/23/lessons-learned-from-selfless-leadership/?sh=43955b112c23.

Schippers, Michaéla C., Deanne N. Den Hartog, Paul L. Koopman, and Daan van Knippenberg. "The Role of Transformational Leadership in Enhancing Team Reflexivity." *Human Relations* 61, no. 11 (2008): 1593–1616.

Seligman, Martin E. P. "Can Happiness Be Taught?." *Daedalus* 133, no. 2 (2004): 80–87.

Seligman, Martin E. P., and Mihaly Csikszentmihalyi. "Positive Psychology: An Introduction." *American Psychologist* 55, no. 1 (2000): 5.

Vernon, Marlo M., E. Andrew Balas, and Shaher Momani. "Are University Rankings Useful to Improve Research? A Systematic Review." *PLOS One* 13, no. 3 (2018): e0193762.

Wilson, R. Coleen, Jeannette T. Crenshaw, and Patricia S. Yoder-Wise. "Call to Action: Prioritizing Reflective Practices for Leadership Success." *Nurse Leader* 20, no. 3 (2022): 258–264.

Zhu, Jinlong, Zhenyu Liao, Kai Chi Yam, and Russell E. Johnson. "Shared Leadership: A State-of-the-Art Review and Future Research Agenda." *Journal of Organizational Behavior* 39, no. 7 (2018): 834–852. https://doi.org/10.1002/job.2296.

# ACT ONE

Clance, Pauline Rose, and Suzanne A. Imes. "The Imposter Phenomenon in High Achieving Women: Dynamics and Therapeutic Intervention." *Psychotherapy: Theory, Research & Practice* 15, no. 3 (1978): 241–247.

Shamir, Boas, and Galit Eilam. "'What's Your Story?' A Life-Stories Approach to Authentic Leadership Development." *The Leadership Quarterly* 16, no. 3 (2005): 395–417.

"Type I and Type II Errors." Wikipedia. Accessed September 12, 2023. https://en.wikipedia.org/wiki/Type_I_and_type_II_errors.

"What Is Purpose-Driven Leadership?" Sidecar Global. Accessed September 12, 2023. https://sidecarglobal.com/.

Zheng, Wei, Alyson Meister, and Brianna Barker Caza. "The Stories That Make Us: Leaders' Origin Stories and Temporal Identity Work." *Human Relations* 74, no. 8 (2021): 1178–1210.

# ACT TWO

"Abraham Lincoln's First Inaugural Address." Wikipedia. https://en.wikipedia.org/wiki/Abraham_Lincoln%27s_first_inaugural_address.

Bracht, Eva M., Fong T. Keng-Highberger, Bruce J. Avolio, and Yiming Huang. "Take a 'Selfie': Examining How Leaders Emerge from Leader Self-Awareness, Self-Leadership, and Self-Efficacy." *Frontiers in Psychology* 12 (2021): 653.

Burnford, Joy. "Limiting Beliefs: What Are They and How Can You Overcome Them?" *Forbes*. January 30, 2019. Accessed September 13, 2023. https://www.forbes.com/sites/joyburnford/2019/01/30/limiting-beliefs-what-are-they-and-how-can-you-overcome-them/?sh=6683de5b6303.

Canfield, Jack, and Mark Victor Hansen. *Dare to Win: The Guide to Getting What You Want Out of Life*. New York: Penguin, 1996.

Canfield, Jack, and Pamela Bruner. *Tapping into Ultimate Success: How to Overcome Any Obstacle and Skyrocket Your Results*. Carlsbad: Hay House, Inc., 2012.

Collins, James C. *Good to Great: Why Some Companies Make the Leap and Others Don't*. New York: Harper Business, 2001.

Cummings, Stephen, Todd Bridgman, and Kenneth G. Brown. "Unfreezing Change as Three Steps: Rethinking Kurt Lewin's Legacy for Change Management." *Human Relations* 69, no. 1 (2016): 33–60. https://doi.org/10.1177/0018726715577707.

Day, David V. "Leadership Development: A Review in Context." *The Leadership Quarterly* 11, no. 4 (2000): 581–613.

De Janasz, Suzanne C., and Monica L. Forret. "Learning the Art of Networking: A Critical Skill for Enhancing Social Capital and Career Success." *Journal of Management Education* 32, no. 5 (2008): 629–650.

Drescher, Marcus A., M. Audrey Korsgaard, Isabell M. Welpe, Arnold Picot, and Rolf T. Wigand. "The Dynamics of Shared Leadership: Building Trust and Enhancing Performance." *Journal of Applied Psychology* 99, no. 5 (2014): 771.

Drucker, Peter. *Managing in the Next Society*. Oxfordshire: Routledge, 2012.

Drucker, Peter. "The American CEO." 2004. https://www.wsj.com/articles/SB110436476581112426.

Drucker, Peter. "The Coming of the New Organization." 1988. *Harvard Business Review*.

Drucker, Peter. *The Practice of Management*. New York: Harper & Brothers, 1954.

Dumas, Colette, and Richard H. Beinecke. "Change Leadership in the 21st Century." *Journal of Organizational Change Management* 31, no. 4 (2018): 867–876.

Erwin, Dennis G., and Andrew N. Garman. "Resistance to Organizational Change: Linking Research and Practice." *Leadership & Organization Development Journal* 31 (2009): 39–56.

Fondas, Nanette, and Margarethe Wiersema. "Changing of the Guard: The Influence of CEO Socialization on Strategic Change." *Journal of Management Studies* 34, no. 4 (1997): 561–584.

Gill, Roger. "Change Management—or Change Leadership?." *Journal of Change Management* 3, no. 4 (2002): 307–318.

Hamilton, Frank, and Cynthia J. Bean. "The Importance of Context, Beliefs and Values in Leadership Development." *Business Ethics: A European Review* 14, no. 4 (2005): 336–347.

Lewin, Kurt. "Frontiers in Group Dynamics: Concept, Method and Reality in Social Science; Social Equilibria and Social Change." *Human Relations* 1 (1947): 5–41.

Mayfield, Jacqueline, and Milton Mayfield. "Leader Communication Strategies Critical Paths to Improving Employee Commitment." *American Business Review* 20, no. 2 (2002): 89–94.

Mind Tools Content Team. "Lewin's Change Management Model: Understanding the Three Stages of Change." Mind Tools. https://www.mindtools.com/ajm9l1e/lewins-change-management-model.

Pearce, Craig L., Bob G. Wood, and Christiana L. Wassenaar. "The Future of Leadership in Public Universities: Is Shared Leadership the Answer?." *Public Administration Review* 78, no. 4 (2018): 640–644.

"Servant Leadership." Wikipedia. Last modified February 2023. https://en.wikipedia.org/wiki/Servant_leadership.

Silva, Alberto. "What Is Leadership?." *Journal of Business Studies Quarterly* 8, no. 1 (2016): 1.

Straub, Richard. "A Time to Rediscover Peter F. Drucker." 2009. http://www.druckersociety.at/files/reaching-out-coming-home.pdf.

"The Project Management Life Cycle: A Complete Guide." Mind Tools. https://www.mindtools.com/pages/article/newPPM_94.htm.

# ACT THREE

"Address at Rice University on the Nation's Space Effort." John F. Kennedy Presidential Library and Museum. Accessed September 8, 2023. https://www.jfklibrary.org/learn/about-jfk/historic-speeches/address-at-rice-university-on-the-nations-space-effort.

Burnes, Bernard, Mark Hughes, and Rune T. By. "Reimagining Organisational Change Leadership." *Leadership* 14, no. 2 (2018): 141–158.

Elkington, Robert, and Jennifer Moss Breen. "How Senior Leaders Develop Resilience in Adversity: A Qualitative Study." *Journal of Leadership, Accountability & Ethics* 12, no. 4 (2015).

Kotter, John P. "Leading Change: Why Transformation Efforts Fail." *Harvard Business Review* 73, no. 2 (1995): 59–67.

NASA Home Page. https://er.jsc.nasa.gov/seh/ricetalk.htm.

Pausch, Randy, and Jeffrey Zaslow. *The Last Lecture.* New York: Hyperion, 2008.

"Resilience." Accessed September 13, 2023. https://www.psychologytoday.com/us/basics/resilience.

Robbins, Tony. *Awaken the Giant Within.* New York: Simon and Schuster, 2012.

Team Tony. "Adopt an Empowering Morning Ritual." Accessed September 13, 2023. https://www.tonyrobbins.com/mind-meaning/ whats-your-morning-ritual/.

"The Last Lecture." Wikipedia. Accessed September 13, 2023, https:// en.wikipedia.org/wiki/The_Last_Lecture.

## ACT FOUR

Cameron, Kim. "Responsible Leadership as Virtuous Leadership." *Journal of Business Ethics* 98 (2012): 25–35.

Harter, Jim. "US Employee eEngagement Needs a Rebound in 2023." Gallup. Accessed January 20, 2023. https://www.gallup.com/ workplace/468233/employee-engagement-needs-rebound-2023.aspx.

SHRM. "How to Fix Poor Employee Engagement." Accessed September 13, 2023. https://www.shrm.org/resourcesandtools/hr-topics/employee-relations/pages/howto-fix-poor-employee-engagement.aspx.

Lanaj, Klodiana, Remy E. Jennings, Susan J. Ashford, and Sathish Krishnan. "When Leader Self-Care Begets Other Care: Leader Role Self-Compassion and Helping at Work." *Journal of Applied Psychology* 107, no. 9 (2022): 1543.

Reagan, Ronald. "Remarks at a Meeting of the White House Conference for a Drug-Free America." Reagan Foundation. Accessed September 13, 2023. https://www.reaganfoundation.org/ronald-reagan/reagan-quotes-speeches/remarksat-a-meeting-of-the-white-house-confer-ence-for-a-drug-free-america/.

Russell, Joyce E. "Positive Leadership: It Makes a Difference." *Forbes.* May 29, 2021. https://www.forbes.com/sites/joyceearussell/2021/05/29/ positive-leadership-it-makes-a-difference/?sh=4c20a967d7a4.

Sinek, Simon. *Start with Why: How Great Leaders Inspire Everyone to Take Action.* New York: Penguin, 2011.

Wayne, John. "John Wayne Quotes." https://www.brainyquote.com/quotes/john_wayne_161631.


# ACT FIVE

De Janasz, Suzanne, and Maury Peiperl. "CEOs Need Mentors Too." *Harvard Business Review* (2015): 4.

Frost, Robert. "Stopping by Woods on a Snowy Evening." Poetry Foundation. Accessed September 13, 2023. https://www.poetryfoundation.org/poems/42891/stopping-by-woods-on-a-snowyevening.

Hersey, Paul, and Kenneth H. Blanchard. "Life Cycle Theory of Leadership". *Training and Development Journal* 23, no. 5 (1969): 26–34.

Hersey, Paul, Kenneth H. Blanchard, and Dewey E. Johnson. *Management of Organizational Behavior—Utilizing Human Resources*. Hoboken: Prentice Hall, 1969.

Kouzes, James M., and Barry Z. Posner. "Leadership Begins with an Inner Journey." *Leader to Leader* 2011, no. 60 (2011): 22–27.

Markham, Steven E., Francis J. Yammarino, William D. Murry, and Michael E. Palanski. "Leader–Member Exchange, Shared Values, and Performance: Agreement and Levels of Analysis Do Matter." *The Leadership Quarterly* 21, no. 3 (2010): 469–480.

McGraw, Tim. "Humble and Kind Lyrics." Genius. Accessed September 13, 2023. https://genius.com/Tim-mcgraw-humble-and-kind-lyrics.

Michie, Susan. "Pride and Gratitude: How Positive Emotions Influence the Prosocial Behaviors of Organizational Leaders." *Journal of Leadership & Organizational Studies* 15, no. 4 (2009): 393–403.

Sivanathan, Niro, Kara A. Arnold, Nick Turner, and Julian Barling. "Positive Psychology in Practice." In *Leading Well: Transformational Leadership and*

*Well-being*, edited by Linley, P. Alex, 241–255. Hoboken: John Wiley & Sons, Inc., 2012. https://doi.org/10.1002/9780470939338.ch15.

"Standing on the Shoulders of Giants." Wikipedia. Accessed September 12, 2023. https://en.wikipedia.org/wiki/Standing_on_the_shoulders_of_giants.

"When Is Your Memory Truly Forgotten?" Legacy Multimedia. Accessed September 13, 2023. https://legacymultimedia.com/when-is-your-memory-truly-forgotten.

# ACKNOWLEDGMENTS

Zac Brown Band. "Highway 20 Ride Lyrics," Genius. Accessed September 20, 2023. https://genius.com/Zac-brown-band-highway-20-ride-lyrics.